MW01710200

Writers Reading at Sweetwaters

An Anthology of Poetry and Prose

Writers Reading at Sweetwaters

EDITORS: CHRIS LORD AND ESTHER HURWITZ

Many thanks to the following contributors:

Zachary Baker
Scott Beal
Carol Bone
Sue Budin
Judith Calleja
Marilyn E. Churchill
Shutta Crum
Lonnie Hull DuPont
Katherine Edgren
Robert Fanning
Larry Francis
Peggy Gray
Don Hewlett
Esther Hurwitz
Kawita Kandpal
Jeff Kass
Mary Jeselnick Koral
Vicki Lawrence
Chris Lord
Chris Moriarty
Michael Moriarty
Edward Morin
Christine Rhein
Veronica Sanitate
Laszlo Slomovits
Sandor Slomovits
Doug Smith
Rick Solomon
Kristin Stelter
Alison Swan
Keith Taylor
Brad Tompkins
Cristina Trapani-Scott
Suzanne Van Appledorn
Thomas Zimmerman
Charles Zwinak

Special thanks to Charles Zwinak for designing the cover.

© 2007 by Word'n Woman Press

All rights reserved by Word'n Woman Press, and
the authors, who retain all copyright to their own material.

Published December 2007
by Word'n Woman Press

Cover art by Charles Zwinak
Design by Chris Lord and Esther Hurwitz
Drawings by Don Hewlett

Word'n Woman Press
Ann Arbor, Michigan 48103
wordnwomanpress@comcast.net

ISBN: 978-0-9795404-1-7

To you, our writers

and

to you, our readers

CONTENTS

Introduction

Chris Lord, Publisher and Editor

We invite you to join us in this print edition of Writers Reading at Sweetwaters, a monthly reading series at Sweetwaters Coffee & Tea in Ann Arbor, Michigan. We thank the founders of Sweetwaters, Lisa and Wei Bee, for offering their establishment for the reading. Featured each month is a respected local writer. Following the feature, writers in the audience read their works.

So pull up a chair, dip your "comma cookie[1]" into steaming coffee, and read/listen with your eyes and heart to the poems and prose written by our authors aged 15 to 75. Cristina Trapani-Scott's "Sewing Pins and Salamanders" poem slips hope under our skin, and holds it there. Kristin Stelter, in her youth, writes ageless poems that forgive. Michael Moriarty gives us visual words that overlay old images with new ones. Larry Francis gives us a photo we will frame. Mary Jeselnick Koral opens her heart in her memoir to let us see the reality and danger of unconditional love, and saves us with her wisdom. Veronica Sanitate makes us sheer and we revel in our own transparency. Sandor Slomovits gives us the wisdom of his daughter Emily, and Laszlo Slomovits tells us the time is now. Alison Swan heats the water of the Great Lakes in her grandmother's kettle, and pours it over Keith Taylor's parched autumn. Rick Solomon teaches us to "speak sensory," and rocks the cocaine-addicted baby. We believe you will find yourself in these writings and savor the experience. Welcome to this issue.

---

[1] A comma cookie is a piece of a cookie cut in the shape of a comma which is a token of appreciation given to every reader.

and Esther Hurwitz, Editor

The first time I performed poetry in public was at an outdoor bar on a bank of the Cuyahoga River in Cleveland. It was a women's open mic event and all a poet had to do was pick a slot and sign up. I scheduled myself for the third round so I could have enough time to observe what the others were doing. In addition to watching the readers, I found myself gazing intently at the freighters floating by, following the progress of sculling teams as they glided down the channel, and swaying with the seagulls wheeling overhead. By the time my turn came, I knew exactly what to do: introduce myself, give the poem's title, indicate that the poem was done, and say, "Thank You" at the end of my set so the audience would know when to applaud. As I stood behind the microphone and looked out at the crowd, I realized that everyone would be paying as much attention to me as I had been paying to them. As I began to speak, I could feel my words being sucked into a wind tunnel.

Some months later, I related this story to my then boyfriend as I was preparing to move back to Ann Arbor, where most poetry events involved speaking poetry out loud. He told me that the next time I got up to read, I should read the most intimate revealing poem I had so I could get it out of the way, and never again have to be embarrassed or nervous about reading. The next time I read out loud, I did exactly that, and you know, he was right. Ever after, I have felt less intimidated.

One of the things Chris and I do with Writers Reading at Sweetwaters is make sure poets of all skill levels feel welcomed. And we couldn't have planned a better audience either. Each month, the connection between readers and listeners is palpable in the room, and because of this our open mic continues to grow.

So now, we'd like to share with you the works of some of our favorite local writers—people whose work we've become quite fond of over this past year. We hope you will enjoy getting to know them too.

Don Hewlett

Sweetwaters Coffee & Tea

Esther Hurwitz

Poetry Should

Poetry should
gently smack you upside the head when
    you've spent too many hours staring at the computer,
or make you go out to play when you'd rather
    sit home reading a book.
She should take you dancing with the angels
    on the head of a pin or
send you on long walks that have no meaning
    even when you get to the end.

Poetry should
sneak you out of the symphony to drink coffee and
    stay up talking all night long,
kiss you with her mouth open and
    leave her panties at home,
make you feel naked
    when explaining herself without words,
and admit that she's slept with Bob Dylan at least twice.

You both should
hop a freight train and bring back stories about the people
    inside the cars
    instead of where the train went.
Then drive to Montana because neither of you
    has ever been there before,
    traveling straight through the night without cruise control
    but with the radio blasting.

On the way back, Poetry should
    remind you that you once relied on training wheels,
then drop you in the desert
    without a compass or canteen.
But she'll have margaritas waiting for you
    when you get back
And you'll have learned to always follow the Northern Star.

Poetry should look you in the eye,
    no matter how many times you've told that story before,
grab the reins from your hands
    and free the ponies,
cover the mirrors and throw out the watches,
    then teach you to sing higher than dogs can hear.

Poetry should
burst in your mouth like a strawberry
    the first time you ate one,
turn you into something more intricate
    than a hand-carved puzzle box,
fill your head with dreams
    even while you're awake,
and hold your hand until the room stops spinning.

Lonnie Hull DuPont

At first she sees the fog as a shroud

settling over the fields of beans, but
she does not wish to start this day
with such a word. She could say the fog
is like muslin stretched over the mouth
of a jelly jar, or it could be like
the birth caul covering a newborn calf
before its mother licks it clean.
It could be like the clouds
in the calico's old eyes —
no, not that. Let it be the caul.
The bean fields, like a baby calf,
are born again this morning,
and the sun will lick them clean.

After Lonnie Hull DuPont and her husband moved into a pre-Civil War farmhouse on the oldest road in Michigan, Lonnie began writing a collection of poems about a fictitious woman living in the house. These two poems are from that collection.

Lonnie Hull DuPont

ON THE SECOND DAY OF FOG, SHE GOES TO MEET IT

sits on the broad root of a broken down
apple tree, remembers being a child
in such fog, searching for fairy houses.
She hears movement in the grass,
keeps very still while the veil of haze
rises to treetops bronzed
by the burn of the sun. Slowly
horses and deer appear all around her,
they graze close together,
nosing fallen apples,
until she forgets
this is still a fallen world.

Vicki Lawrence

INCUBUS (EXCERPT)

I dreamed the same dream all during my childhood, over and over in a hundred variations, all in black and white, like the newsreels at the movies on Saturday afternoons. The black sky, the pale line of the horizon, the gray, flat lie of the land. Tiny buildings, trees, a white fence. Then it comes, black against black, the roiling cloud suddenly extruding an obscene tail that dips and withdraws, dips, dips. It touches, trails, idly doodling its way across the landscape like the finger of God, raising a pillar of dust wherever it touches. It grows larger, feeding on houses. It sucks in cars and trees. It is a howling giant nosing about the land, searching. It comes closer, and the white fence shatters. It grows bigger and bigger, searching and searching.

My screams would wake the house, but not me. I was in the grip of the storm, my voice lost in the shrieking of the wind. Only slowly would I become aware that the shrieking was mine, that my mother was holding me, rocking me, murmuring, over and over, "You're all right, baby. You're all right. Wake up, sweetie. You're all right." My face was wet with tears. My arms were around her neck, tight.

She tried to keep me from it, but the book also held me in thrall. I loved the story, loved all the Oz books, but I knew that picture was there. The cloud filled the page, black on black, the funnel curving down toward the corner, Dorothy's house, tiny, white, frail, spinning helplessly up into ever thicker coils of black. I thought about it, thought about that black thing on the page, waiting. I demanded to see it, my hands clenched, white. And we sat down together as I slowly turned the pages, knowing it was coming, knowing exactly how many pages there were to go. Sometimes I couldn't stand it. I slammed the book shut and wouldn't look. Other times I would turn the page, my fingers trembling, and see it. Sometimes I cried. Sometimes I couldn't.

I've looked at all the family photos from those years, all in black and white, till it seems to me that even my memories have faded, the colors all leached out. I see my dad as he is in the snapshots, young, strong, thin, wearing his old leather flight jacket and standing proudly in front of his new 1953 Ford station wagon. My mother I see at her daintiest, dressed in a short-sleeved sweater, a long, full skirt, and pearls, seated in the big armchair at her parents' house in town. She is smiling self-consciously into the camera, her lips full and dark against her pale skin as she holds my baby brother up to the camera. I see me playing in the plastic wading pool, absorbed, alone, my hair long and dark and tangled, my bathing suit a wet gray, the house and fence white behind me.

~

I was four when the tornado came. I remember the day. I have reconstructed it, played it over and over in my mind, till the memory has become grooved and worn and inflexible, like an old phonograph record, heavy and brittle and black.

Time passed slowly that morning. My mother, always cleaning, got a load of wash out onto the line, apparently hoping the clouds gathering over the dark, flat fields to the west would hold off. My baby brother was fussy and took all the attention she could spare from the laundry. The sun ducked behind the clouds, casting the house into shades of gray, and then popped out again. The wind began to murmur in the trees, the tiny new leaves trembling against the branches.

After lunch I battled not to have to take a nap. I lay on the couch, my eyes not shut, my heart black with anger. Clouds filled the sky. In my parents' room my brother fussed in his crib. A gust of air sent the Venetian blinds singing and swaying and then swept over my bare legs. It felt thin and cold and nasty. I was suddenly afraid.

My mother walked around the little house, jiggling my brother on her shoulder and patting his behind. I followed along, brushing against her as we walked. The wind buzzed through the doorframe and the windows rattled. We were back in the living room when we heard a thunk and a rumble outside.

My mother hurried toward the kitchen, my brother wailing in her arms. I clutched at her skirt. She pulled herself free and went out, firmly shutting the screen door between us. I sobbed against it.

She ran down the steps, the wind blowing her skirt and hair out before her as she hurried down the long narrow yard under a flat, weird sky. Snapping in the wind, the clothes on the line were tearing themselves free. Behind me the windows chattered and laughed, saying terrible things. The wind rapped and pounded at them, trying to get at me. The light turned queasy and evil.

"Momma!" I cried. I reached above my head and turned the handle. The door ripped itself from my grasp and banged against the porch wall. I stood astounded as it banged back again, barely missing me. It whipped open again, and I ran out, yelling for her. I raced down the three steps and stepped into a river of wind. It pushed and carried me along. Suddenly, it scooped my feet from under me.

My scream pierced the air. My mother whirled around just as the wind threw me, hard, against the picket fence. She stood a split second in amazement, my brother in one arm, a handful of shirts in the other, hair and clothes streaming behind her. Then she dropped the shirts, just let them whip away, and ran to me.

We battled to regain the house. My mother, crouched low, fought against the wind step by step, one arm pressing the baby to her chest, her hand splayed against his neck and head, the other wrapped around me on her hip, as I clung, monkey-like, my arms wrapped around her neck, tight. Over her shoulder I saw the huge oak at the back of the yard, bending and tossing its head as though in pain, smacking its lower limbs to free it of my family's clothes. Ahead of us the screen door banged and writhed on its hinges. One end ripped itself free, and, as we reached the bottom step, the other went. We crouched in the lee of the porch as the door knocked its way over the railing. Then my mother ran for the gaping doorway.

Inside it was dark. The windows glowed like great eyes. We stood in the kitchen and gasped in the thick air, feeling the great wind sigh and suck around the building. The house seemed to exhale, and with a high sharp crack every window burst out into a flying field of glass. Then we heard it, lower and deeper than the noise all around us—like a freight train rumbling toward us, like a plane roaring to takeoff, like a mountain rumbling and trembling as it rips itself open, louder and louder.

My mother's breath caught in her throat. My sobs turned back into screams. Clasping us close, she dashed through the house, the roar of the wind ratcheting ever lower and louder. She ran into the bedroom and threw the baby down on the bed. His crying turned high-pitched and hysterical. She knelt down and pulled me off her, wrenching my arms free as I shrieked, my pale hands grabbing for her in the wan light, wet and sticky with blood that shone black. She shoved me under the bed, pushed in my brother on a pillow, and then slid under herself. I grabbed her and the three of us clung together as the house rocked and shook and our screams were sucked into the great black shrieking terror all around us.

Doug Smith

EAST ON HIGHWAY 117

Driving through pine and spruce
down a sandy two lane highway
in the District of Muskoka, Ontario
my ears pop as the car rises
off the asphalt and races down
a deserted blushing sumac hill.
I'm listening to the Rolling Stones
...you can't always get...
I stick a piece of plum into my mouth
...what you want...
pass a pear to my son
...but if you try sometime...
before the sun disappears
behind a row of trees
...you just may find...
the crickets sleep, the night breathes
...you'll get what you need...
I park the car beside a cold campfire,
headlights fragment into fog
adrift from the lake, lights scatter
ghostly into the forest around me.
A loon's song keeps time
with the dog's snore, his head
in the lap of my sleeping son.
I pull the bottle out of the bag,
unscrew the cap, stick the whiskey
between my legs, roll down
the window, look for stars up
through a canopy of branches,
hear again the hiccupy staccato,
wonder will it take the whole bottle
to admit she was right?

Doug Smith

REXROTH AT THE WINDOW

Morning sun breathes through windows
whispers lost stanzas adrift in an old house
where children recite tales of a secret door
open to fields the hue not found on
an artist's pallet, there is no explanation,
tomorrow I receive an award for work
I don't remember writing.

Safe now in overstuffed chair near dormer
daughters gather around me, happy nymphs
of a Midsummer's Night's Dream singing
"You are my sunshine, my only sunshine."
Despite their nearness I strain to hear them,
in their arms this sorrow will not leave me
staring out the window onto barren fields,
a brown landscape without definition, divided
by a river too cold and deep to swim across.

The screen door flaps wildly in the wind
jars me from reflection in the window.
I hear horses pace in their stalls or is it
the pole barn roof creaking, breathing?
Rain strafes the leafless giant maple,
bends an oak tree into prayer,
dogs chase a rabbit into a prickly thicket,
their squeals mix with the thunder
into a joyless chorus. I see ghosts
on whose shoulders I stand, their lucent
woeful faces wincing from the burden.
"All for poetry?"
their expressions seem to ask.

This ought to be the last season
I walk in these shoes.
Next year I will throw away my clothes
and walk along the stony beaches
                    of Poros,
a man without enemies
          a man without friends,
chasing small luminous fish
in the shallow Mediterranean waters
looking for the axis of the world
to surface from the coarse white sand.

Like the novice prays for humility,
like the Bodhisattva seeks great compassion,
I know this kind of madness must be earned.

Katherine Edgren

MORNING ON CASS LAKE

I covet a glimpse of the wildness that nests nearby,
conductor of daily patrols of its blue-green domain.
I dip and pull through shallows and dappling shadows,
relish the widening rings of minnows that scatter,
the vortices drawn by skittering water striders,
and the glistening of the wild rice beyond the reeds.

The kayak paddle grants me long arms, a long glide.
My wrists trace figure eights in the bug-free air.
Beyond Buck's, past the tall pines, close to shore
there's a short cry, a stirring, and the eagle apparates
like a cross pinned to the sky. White head and tail,
dark body outlined against cosmic blue.

Good morning, old pajama wearer, Minnesota denizen,
thermal hanger! Wings tilt and hold like oars.
We stare up or down in cradles of sky and lake,
as all around us life scatters and skitters
and glistens. For mere seconds, we levitate
and the air and water lose their separateness.

Katherine Edgren

Fourth of July

Hanging with my posse of new & re-discovered friends
having a drink or two, thinking about sunk costs
& types of fireworks & connections between the two
& connections between any two seemingly disparate things
& how something beautiful is often inexplicable & vice-versa &
how I continue to mourn the loss of her & him & him—
even though it's been years & I've already begun to mourn the loss
of all those who are leaving, & how we invest years, work
dedication, hopes, the details of our lives, every fiber of our being
to get to a point where all is lost, seemingly for nothing—
but not really—or we would never have reached this point
filled with this experience & now this hard-won wisdom,
        & how it's really
only the future we have left, & how this epiphany
        of the fallacy of sunk costs
is like a kind of a firework & I'm trying to figure out exactly what kind
but when I Google "types of fireworks," all I get are legal ones
& I want to know the names of the illegal ones,
        which probably have names like
needle fire, because this realization is huge & probably illegal & deserves
an illegal fireworks name, & it's funny & amazing how the
two things are connected & the whole inevitable sadness
        of life envelops &
threatens to overwhelm me & I consider jumping off something
& I search for fresh revelations, & reach out to friends,
because they've been there too
& there's this big circle of comfort, each one getting & giving, &
it's all connected, tears & fears, & we become
a part of each other's memories that sometimes leak into daily lives
& I know the pain will eventually
go underground, but first I must "do the time" & sink into it
& be resentful & angry, go through denial, while
packing in fresh experiences, looking back at all the subtleties
unappreciated at the time, & try to stop thinking about it
when I first wake up, & have another drink or two
with my posse of new and re-discovered friends
despite rain on a holiday & tiredness on a weekend night
and all the aches and pains of aging
because it's life & possessing & strangely beautiful.

Zachary Baker

July 4th, 2007

Stars and stripes
    backlit by ochre cascading night.

Adjacent atop a building of bricks
    a light shines omnipresent—illuminescent
        in halogen religious rapture
            to the rag rapping in the wind.

Back nearest the light
    bugs scream their mad flight
        burning their death
            as the stars in the heavens behind them.

But no matter
    I squeeze your hand
        and you squeeze back
            we think of fireworks (in our own
                gender-specific way).

Nothing is behind us
Nothing in front of us
'cept this stage
all the world.

Zachary Baker

WAKING

Revolving summer
The red dust of the late sun
And the sugarplums

Thomas Zimmerman

LABOR DAY

Back-deck umbrella shade
        bathes the page
I sack my soul
        to seek a sage   meet a mage

A king's ransom's what
        my waking mind will pay
for a peep into
that valley   cleft   fjord   Naples Bay
        of image   thought   rhythm   song   lay

Three birds
        fly chirping overhead
        My beer bottle sweats
                The air conditioner hums

Patience   silence
                Something
                might be coming

Sartre said
        there are no geniuses
only works
        of genius

Summer's end
        An orange cat
        stalks across the backyard grass
Why can't I follow her
mewing   on my hands and knees

        Whine of tires on I-94
        Harley snarl   Porsche snort
                pass on by   leave me blind

When I need a poem the most
                that is when it hides

Thomas Zimmerman

MEMORY PRESENT

Stubble-bearded   muddle-headed
here
he begins again

Leonard Cohen   Mose Allison
on the stereo

It's been months
since he's seen her legs

            The last time
            it was *Pietá* all over again
                        The woman takes
                        a broken man   makes him
                        whole again

            Red wine in a black glass
            Barking late-night Chocolate Lab
            Ecstasy and tears
            Unfamiliar sheets

No photos
Nothing public
Only part of a poem

She's a minority
He's white and male and conspicuously free

Something (maybe the TV) tells him
he should be sorry
            for the present
            as well as the memory

Scott Beal

Creative Movement

Ms. flashes the pink page as the music kindles
and I crane my petals toward the fluorescents,
turning slowly, I bow and exchange
yes-you're-a-wonderful-flower smiles
with a girl clinging to her mothers' legs
as the bolder kids shriek and pound
bare feet on the wood floor—get it, *wild*flowers—
and my head is buzzing not with hangover,
not with stress, but with the overgrown bees
overgrown flowers draw, and which we become
as Ms. turns the yellow page, we dart
in circles poking our noses into the invisible
beds from which I suppose we've just been uprooted,
which makes us a little jittery
so the purple page quells us into butterflies,
I shush and am shushed then we glide
with arms swishing, and if we were
really butterflies we would be the world's most graceless
butterflies, gardeners would smack us with trowels
but we omit this bit from the act for the blue page
whisks us into wind howling clockwise through the meadow,
a sour breeze laden with the sweat and fungus
of the morning yoga class, and when the red page makes us rain,
we pitterpatter and wiggle
our fingers like mad and not one juice-sticky face
rinses clean before the white page shines
in Ms.'s hand to freeze us to soft flakes, we drift to the ground
and wave our arms and legs to make angels
against the grain of the hardwood, then rise
for the brown page which in the class's weird chronology
means it's time for the flower to shrivel back to the floor
until we lie scattered and akimbo across the room
as though the entire class has been mown down, we lie still
as Ms. cuts the lights and the brown page flutters in the fan.

Eyes close. The ceiling whirls. Floorboards slacken
and the class sinks into brown depths—
not seeds, not worms—each child and adult locked
in the bone and gristle of ourselves
and I am in the moment
as the soil mounds over us, packing the space
between teeth and tongue
while microbes thin us to less than ash.
Thoughts trickle through bedrock,
the last flickers of private systems in which every lemon,
every brakelight drums in the limbs. The dinner plate
waves the green page stinking of peas, the crumpled
red page covers a parent's face, a flat screen blinks
through gray pages dense with data, and each jolts
a specific cowering, the shadows of which
now drain into the water table, cool and still.
Then Ms. raises the pink page
and we shoot into our floral selves again,
even the shy girls now craze the garden with palms
and cheeks, knuckles and bruises in garish clashes,
and my head goes on buzzing
after the last color is spent.

Charles Zwinak

WHAT MAKES A MARRIAGE

Sitting under a tree alone
is not a bad start
as being alone is not.

She sits under a tree
so far away that I
can only see the tree
as a tree-shape against the sky.

I cannot see her
but I know, not only
that she sits, but
how she sits
one ankle over the other
glasses resting open
on her lower thigh.

What's more
I know she knows that I am here
and how I am sitting.

We sit under two trees
an apple and a pine—
which is under which
is between her and me.
This is not a forest
but two trees widely spaced
on a cool green plain
seeded and tended by a pro.

We do not
expect to learn to float
ankles on knees
or have an ideal apple
or cone, knock us on the crown
like a Newton or an Eve.
We are only too glad
to remain uncrowned.

Here, there is a sky
full of birds singing
though there is no
need to be sung to.

Early on, we taught
ourselves to whistle
a similar, but notice
I do not say
            the same song.

From time to time
we sit and whistle
or listen to the bird's
singing, as birds, too
have always sung
sometimes together
more often
            alone.

Marilyn E. Churchill

SOLACE

It's a starry night and there's a nearly full moon making the snow glisten. After celebrating our son Owen's twenty-fifth birthday in Kalamazoo, we have driven back to the park to look for the cell phone he has lost. Since it wasn't at the restaurant, it's got to be here where he ran his dog before sundown. At his request, under "contacts," I press "Owen" on my cell, and lo, there's a distant ringing in the field. He follows it, reaches down, plucks his phone from deep in the snow and returns to the car, beaming. He's both lucky and smart, I think.

On the way back to Ann Arbor, my husband Jay and I listen to the folk show "The Thistle and Shamrock" with Fiona Ritchie. It's a good tired I feel having "done" the birthday and listening to mellow music while being mesmerized by the night sky. When we finally pull in the driveway about 9:30, there's just letting the cat out, since he's been cooped up all day. Now that both our sons have left home for jobs, he's my sole charge.

Off he goes, cat legs moving so fast they're hardly visible, along the snowy sidewalk, probably off to find his friend. After about fifteen minutes I manage to trick him into coming in, but soon he's grousing noisily about the raw deal and against my better judgment, I open the door for him a second time. Stormy is nine years old, he's gray with patches of white on his throat and belly, and he's the first cat Jay has taken a liking to, maybe because he's the first "guy" cat we've had. He can be really annoying when he wants our attention, scratching at the pile of papers on my desk or tearing up newspapers if we get too engrossed in television, but mostly, he's very affectionate and playful. Mr. Personality.

After getting ensconced in reading the Sunday paper, I suddenly remember Stormy at about 10:30 and rush to open the door. Immediately I see something is wrong. There's a dark form on the small piece of snow-covered lawn between the sidewalk and the driveway. A neighbor's cat who is sniffing nearby appears frightened and darts away as I approach. It's definitely Stormy lying there, his tongue hanging out, the snow stained with blood from his mouth. He doesn't move when I stroke his fur. His eyes are open and ice crystals have begun to form over them.

My livewire cat, my companion, my baby I've nursed through a plant poisoning and let out thousands of times, my street savvy cat, is dead. I didn't even hear a car go by this silent, snowy night. I lift his limp body, set it in a cardboard box Jay has brought, and carry the box in the house, even though Stormy won't need protection from the cold. I imagine after he was hit, he crawled or staggered the twenty or so feet towards the house. Inside, my husband and I sob in each other's arms. It's clear to me that Jay also loved Stormy.

In the middle of the night, I'm roused from a deep sleep by the strains of a song emanating from the music box—the one my older sister Kathy gave me, that sits on top of a book shelf in our bedroom. It's pitch black, the clock says 2:00, and I hear the closing bars of the tune, "I'll be loving you, always," with the final faint clink an octave higher. My husband, a sound sleeper, amazingly has also heard it. I haven't wound the box or touched it for months. This has never happened before and probably will never happen again.

The music box is a small, white porcelain dish, with delicate roses on its lid, given to me many years ago by Kathy, who died just over two years ago, in early February, 2005, after having a heart attack during dialysis. At age 62, she was the first of my siblings to pass away. Immediately I am struck by the synchronicity of this event. I have a powerful sense that Kathy, who also loved cats, has sent me, via this music, love and comfort for the loss of Stormy. And perhaps a reminder to think of her often.

The next day I wind up the music box and listen. The tempo is much faster than the song would be played or sung. And of course it slows as it winds down. It's as if the tail end of the song had gotten stuck in there, waiting for the right moment.

Don Hewlett

Cat

Chris Lord

Blue Lint in the Moon's House

Three sparrows weave wind
with the drooping branches of a lilac bush
A house wren, tail upright, chatters its domain
from the top rung of a sloping wood fence
A fledgling sparrow taking an early flight
lands on its mother's back, slides off, beak open
A starling feeds in the seeding grass
casts a black spell over a finch's singing
A mother cardinal leaves the high wire
to drink from a birdbath, plucks the fur
of the cat sleeping under the spirea bush,
carries it to the flowering tree to line its nest

The sun I have waited for is too bright
I lose my way as I stare into its red mirror,
search for what can and cannot be seen
I change my hair but cannot change my face
change houses but not my home
change the clock but time is still the same
I cannot turn back, cannot collect the warm egg
My hands are my grandmother's hands
dipping a freshly killed hen in boiling water

I stalk fledgling memory; the cat stalks the sun
I sit beside the wren on the fence;
a robin, a cardinal splash in the birdbath
The birds cannot see the cat against the wall
I dismantle the wall each day for sun and bird,
find it rebuilt each morning from blocks of night
I lean against it, tired of planting nameless seeds,
know I will not recognize what grows
for I am grown and cannot recognize what matters

Perhaps it is not the light I need to see but what
flowers in the approaching dark, dropping a star
in the cat's mouth, pulling reason behind rain
I listen to the yellow warble scaling the wall,
to the song falling into whispers of grass
I collect the wind's hair for a nest but cannot see
into the small opening in the moon's house
I bring a dragonfly as a gift
wait in silence to be asked in

Peggy Gray

For the Cat (excerpt)

"You know how people are, when they run out of gift ideas, they head right for the pet shop. This might be a big day for the register. All the others had their reasons for not being able to work on Christmas Eve. I sure do appreciate you for staying."

Of course Karen would stay, nothing else to do, not that she would want him to know, so said she had a date but would break it to help him out. He said that would be great, she must have been convincing, or maybe not. It didn't seem to faze him that someone would make such an offer. She didn't care, hadn't bothered with the holidays in many years, no tree or trimmings, bad enough next week it will turn 1950 and she will turn thirty. Watching him put on his coat she thinks how he looks so like the man on the cover of her current romance novel. He puts his hand on the doorknob, then turns back towards her and says, "I'm taking off early. If no one buys that kitten, you can have it for working tonight." Their eyes meet just as a clump of hair comes loose from her bun.

"Oh," she tucks all the strands back behind her ear, "but you already gave me this candy."

The slow creep of embarrassment begins the reddening climb from her toes to the back of her neck around her whole face, setting her ears ablaze as she realizes she is clutching the five-pound box to her chest like she could never give it up. He doesn't seem to notice, just opens the door, still talking.

"That was a Christmas present. This would be a *thank-you* present. I sure do appreciate you working till 9:00 tonight. Besides, you know I don't like to handle cats. We wouldn't have this one if it wasn't free, so if we do sell it, 100% profit, can't beat that, but it probably won't sell, so it's yours if you want it."

As he shuts the door behind him, the clamorous chiming of a string of bells hanging on the knob gets on her nerves and she closes her hand around them to muffle the ringing, stares after him through the glass pane, lets out a sigh and releases her grip.

Snow is just starting, making his black overcoat a fuzzy blur as it moves into the distance. Karen looks over at the scrawny cat. "What makes him think I would want you? No one else does. I'm not allowed to have pets in my flat and I sure can't afford one."

The kitten's mouth opens wide as if to show how small and not that much to feed, letting out something between a meow and a purr. "What kind of cat are you, anyway?" She lifts him out and shakes her head.

"No wonder you were abandoned, this is the first time I've ever seen a kitten that wasn't cute and I wonder if he gave the other employees a gift, wonder if he gave them something new or some straggly stray that someone brought in off the street."

Now it occurs to her that they probably got a box of candy too. Why would she have thought this was a special gift just for her? Oh, she knows why she would have thought it all right; and, of course, his new wife probably did the shopping, bought everyone the same, why would she not? How would she know? Karen looks back out the door but he and his blurry coat have vanished in the white darkness.

"And another thing the snow will do," she always talks out loud to herself when she's alone in the store, "is snarl traffic. Now the bus will be running late, it will take an hour to get home, and the bus driver, John—his name must be John because it says so on his uniform." In all the years she's ridden the same bus she's never called him by his name to his face, nor has he asked hers, even though she always sits behind him and they talk all the way to her stop.

"He'll have more time to remind me about the job opening at the department store where his cousin works." Her voice rises, "He'll want to know if I called the number he gave me."

In all the years Karen's worked here, she's never gotten used to being alone with the little noises. With all the disturbances in a room full of small animals, there are certain creaks and scratchings that scare her even if she knows it's just the building settling, or so they say. The sound of her voice comforts her, covers up any unusual sounds.

"And when I tell John I haven't yet called, he'll start in on asking why wouldn't I want a better paying job, closer to home, where I can meet lots of nice young men."

The bells on the doorknob jangle and her heart jumps, "He did come back." With trembling hands she smoothes back her hair on each side, pushes her glasses up the bridge of her nose, then looks at the kitten who stares back. Eyes like green slits peer up through the matted fur, and she says in a whisper to the cat. "He did come back." The corners of her mouth are quivering, "Hi!"

It's just Beverly and Jeanne, two sixth-graders who often stop in on their way home from school. Usually they are in navy gabardine uniform jumpers. Today, of course, is not a school day. Still, both have on the same slightly wrinkled oxford blouses, but with pink skirts and petticoats, just like twins, even though they're not related at all. Even their coats are alike, bought in different years, Karen knows, Beverly's being a little short in the sleeves, Jeanne's too long, way too big in the shoulders.

Karen remembers her own coat and shoes, always bought several sizes larger in those days to get several years wear out of them, then had to wear them till they were much too small. She can't recall the precise time when things actually fit just right.

"That was different," she thinks, "we were from the Depression days, thought we were lucky just to have coats. These girls' parents, what's their reason?"

The girls are staring at her. Jeanne says, "What?" And Karen realizes that she is talking aloud again and feels the blush starting "I mean, ah, how are your parents this season? We've got some new hamsters if you want to see them." They always want to see whatever animal is new. Two weeks ago they bought a parakeet, after saving their allowances for a month. "How's Tweety?" She thinks that's what they named it.

"We want our money back," Jeanne says.

"Yes, a refund," Beverly chimes in.

"Why?"

"Look, the man gave us a paper that says this bird is guaranteed to talk in one month if you talk to it."

"The man?"

"You know, the nice one, I think he's the owner, he gave us the guarantee." And she can picture him, elbows on the counter, sleeves of his white shirt folded up twice, his dark hair combed back, telling the girls about how to get a bird to talk.

She asks, "Did you talk to it?"

"Yes, but he won't ever talk now."

Jeanne lays the folded guarantee on the counter, unwraps it, and out rolls a dead parakeet.

"Well, now girls, the guarantee said that it would talk, not how long it would live."

"Yes, but if it doesn't live, it can't talk and this says that it will talk."

"Did it talk before it died?"

"No."

"OK, then I'll give you a refund for that." She will give them the money, she decides, and ordinarily she would never make such a decision without calling him to approve it, but it is Christmas Eve and she feels both confident and generous. "Here, want to hold this kitten while I get your refund?"

Both girls, in unison, say "No."

A lump forms in Karen's throat, as she holds the squirming handful onto the shoulder of her smock with one hand and with the other reaches for the bird corpse to dispose of it, but Beverly grabs it first.

"We'll take it. We want to have a funeral."

Karen can't help but feel annoyed with them as the girls try to divide $2.98 equally, twice asking her to make change so it will come out just right. She'd help them figure it out but decides it's a good lesson in arithmetic. Beverly finally puts what she has deemed to be her share in the pocket where she has stuffed the bird and Jeanne asks how much for a hamster because she still needs a gift for her mother. Beverly reminds her that the need for food and a cage makes it way out of her reach and they should walk over to the dime store where there is a great selection of jewelry and they might even have change left for a soda, if there is time, because they will be late getting home if they don't hurry. On their way out, they wind their way around each cage and aquarium, with words of praise for each creature within. But none for the cat. They never look at him, even though Karen had set him down into the prettiest cage, the one with pink and silver ribbons, ready for holiday giving. The bells on the door clang as they leave. The kitten curls up into the corner. Maybe he can't hear, Karen thinks. He didn't react to the door closing or the bells. Out of habit, she reaches under the counter for the vinegar to clean fingerprints off the glass, pauses, then picks the kitten up in both hands.

"You're too plain. Everyone chooses the pretty ones. No one will ever choose us—I mean you." She holds him closer. "You could be pretty if you tried. I'll help you." It occurs to her how much better it is to be talking to someone, even if it is just a cat, rather than herself, and how since she's worked here, never has she talked to any of the other animals, or fish, or anything, barely even the other employees.

"I'll brush you and put ribbons on you. Maybe then someone will notice you. If not, maybe I will keep you. He told me to, after all."

Edward Morin

FEBRUARY

by Cai Qijiao (translators: E. Morin, Dennis Ding, Fang Dai)

Today I must be exceptionally gentle
so I can tell my friends the best of news.
Go on quickly budding your light green leaves—
the season in you already waves its greeting to me.

Here's what the moss in the rain is telling me,
as it appears on top of the drenched walls:
such masses of bright life-giving green
are the sure sign of spring's arrival.

The fingers of the wind caressing my cheek
already seem surprisingly warm and soft,
my throat breathes in currents of moist air
as if drinking the mellowest wine without restraint.

Remember that bright day not long ago
when a butterfly paid a call at my window;
it sipped on a nearly withered winter-plum flower—
upon what hill slope could it be perching now?

I guess the peach trees blooming by the lake
must have watched this splendid parade in their dreams,
for they've hurriedly decked their branches with blossoms,
and greenness pulsates quickly through their boughs.

In ploughed fields all over the countryside
countless bands of sparrows happily frolic;
tranquil mountains that seem to float among the clouds
undulate like swatches of light green silk.

Time to view the colors of spring in the wild,
you my friends who have formed unbreakable ties with spring
in this fine season that belongs to you alone,
what melody of life will you be singing?

Edward Morin

Blue Jays

call "Thief! Thief!" I must
rise early. A nest of them
makes my street a proving ground
for mischief—flower pots
tipped over, barbecues raided,
sleep spoiled. They cruise by
carefree as sharks.

Last year robins lived here—
well-mannered, industrious,
respectful of property.
One street over, cardinals
serenade. Their brownish young
are voluble, elaborate
with the modesty of talented
beginners.

Jays are from the underworld,
sinister as Dutch elm disease.
In high branches, once the dew
burns off, two exchange
piercing rubato lyrics
without a trace of warmth.

Then the whole pack bickers,
turning the neighborhood
into a tenement courtyard.
They won't leave in winter.
They'll stay—accusing each other
and the sparrows who make way
for them at feeding stations.

Until just one is left chattering
for himself against the world
and the bare oaks, crying:
This is home. This is home.

Sue Budin

RUMOR

"Hope is a thing with feathers…"
-Emily Dickinson

Who has seen the ivory bill
of the woodpecker
that like a slice of moon
lights up the swamp?

Some say they've spied it,
sat in boats for hours, binoculars
like insects' eyes

waiting for a white wing
bigger than a crow's
to appear and to hear

the "tick, tick" of its beak
hammering dead wood to
find its prey.

There is a hope that rides
in each of us—to find what others
claim extinct and resurrect it

as the man in his canoe
paddles to movement
in the cypress trees

imagines birds approaching
through the dark woods.

Sue Budin

DRUGSTORE

Lipstick, candy red, vermillion.
Cigars, Old Havana.
Colgate, its Gardol shield protecting my teeth.

I danced on the black polished floors
shiny as Russian lacquered boxes.
My father wore a white gown, not like those of prom girls
floating in a sea of voile but starched white cotton
snapped up to his neck. Quickly, two by two
or three by three, he filled the capsules white—
Digitalis, Belladonna, names for wicked stepmothers,
resourceful daughters.

Outside, trollies rattled by and the bottles danced.
Two red chairs, like glamorous whores,
waited for prescriptions
and would always follow directions.
I arranged rows of shampoo, sundries,
feminine hygiene products whose brands I memorized,
whose purpose I could never understand
until my blood seeped through,
tinged the magic of this hall
where a man in a gown banged a jar.

The compound settled
as I was just beginning to rise up.

Keith Taylor

At the Wendy's East of Saline

for Anne Carson

Behind the back parking lot
of the fast food restaurant,
close to the factory
that makes molded plastic parts—
bumpers, knobs and cup-holders—
for the big Ford pickup truck,
in a scrubby stand of oaks
next to a subdivision
of vinyl-sided houses,
a great horned owl peers
over the edge of her nest,
seemingly unperturbed,
as if she's been watching there
for two or three thousand years.

Keith Taylor

Upper Peninsula Fires

A hundred miles north the forest is burning.
Smoke drifts down this far at night and just at dawn
I smell something like wet charcoal in my cabin.
Sunsets glow deeper red and spectacular
the longer the fire burns, the more jack pine,
second-growth white pine, and cedars in dry swamps
smolder into the autumn of a parched year.

Veronica Sanitate

FALL EXPECTANCY

I.
I awaken early with expectancy, my dreams
swollen and watery. My mind slips out
the hand-hewn door and sails down the long sand
drive toward the silver mailbox where I expect
my life will arrive. It will flow on the breeze
and meet me half-way down the color-changing path.

II.
In the afternoon we watch fall come on. The leaves
purposefully leap into the creek then float down
golden, like solid-state honey. (The gold the pioneers
sought. Gold of place. Color of pure timing.)
They seem eager for the crumbling of their texture
and the swift issue of spirit on downstream dreams.

III.
Tonight, Harry Honey sold his 15 years of bees
and gave us two last jars of his liquid self. Mom
sits on the deck and recollects how she and Dad
planted the twin pines by the creek the day
Lill Bottoms seamlessly slipped into the North Branch
and drowned in the dark of Kellogg's Bridge, down

IV.
Down River Road, altering the flow of things
with her face-down floating self-possession. Maybe
she saw herself as a leaf and leaped, or wanted
to pour her gold out of or into the dream,
or expected to meet herself in the color-bending
stream, her face kissing her original face.

Alison Swan

Grace

It has been sub-zero for days
and our house is snug, sure,
but still . . .

The sky is blue. The snow is
blue too. And if there's green
in those evergreens
I don't see it. Winter.
A hundred days long.

Mid-winter, mid-Michigan
who doesn't love a cardinal?
Something red and quick and loud.
How many Februaries have I
listened for their song
to begin again? The songbirds

who have sacrificed
so very much more than I
float above the trees even today
when the cold is too cold for school.

The cedar hedge scatters sunlight
and I see palm fronds,
bougainvillea.
That even the barest trees
are the perches of birds.

Their hollow bones
make them lighter than air.
Their tiny hearts keep us all
from freezing.

Alison Swan

EXCERPT FROM "THE KETTLE"

The brew pub was dark and cheerful, the air redolent of fresh beer. Next to my husband and me, a huge aquarium full of freshwater fish glowed brown-green. I was appreciating the nod to locality when a young woman poured a plastic bag of water and minnows into the tank. I watched the tiny silver fish dart or hang among the stones and weeds. Most were eaten immediately. One managed to evade capture for several long moments. I silently rooted for it. I am not a lighthearted person; when a bass gobbled it up, my stomach lurched.

"So I'm really going to do it. We're not just going to talk about it. I'm going to go up there and get that kettle." I was cheering myself on.

Dave sipped his pint and nodded. "And whatever else you want."

We'd driven to Kalamazoo's warehouse district through gray January countryside from our new house in Saugatuck, a small town near the Lake Michigan mouth of the Kalamazoo River. Half a dozen Great Lakes fish digested their meal behind glass. Outside, cold winter rain melted the snow cover to slush. And I thought about the little cabins in the woods five hundred miles away near the frozen Lake Superior shore. It was my thirty-sixth birthday, and I was conspiring to smash a window or jimmy the door at somebody else's summer place.

Somebody else's summer place. It makes me cringe now to describe it that way. Fifty years ago, on land owned by his father-in-law on Lake Independence near Big Bay, Michigan, my grandfather converted the cinder-block garage of an old hunting camp into a three-room cabin, a rustic second home where he, my grandmother, my mother, and her four sisters spent summers and some weekends. They lived the rest of the year in Marquette, a small Victorian city perched on the cliffs above Lake Superior. The cabin was just an hour's drive along the coast from home, but it was a world away.

Established by a logging company around 1902, when almost everything or everyone arrived or departed via the notoriously unpredictable waters of Superior, Big Bay never prospered, at least not for more than a few families. It is too remote or buggy or cold, depending upon which local you ask and what the most recent challenge has been. Everyone complains about the isolation, mosquitoes, and weather, but no one who sticks around really doubts that those three things keep the town exactly how they want it: peaceful and plain.

By the early 1970s, when I was a schoolgirl spending summer vacations with my family and grandparents in their cabin, Big Bay had a few paved roads but was absent from state road maps. "We go here," I'd tell curious friends from my downstate home, pointing at an irregular blue pentagon, Lake Independence, the large inland lake that, on a map, looked to be a stone's throw from Superior, at the literal end of the road. There were a few decades around the turn of the last century when transient lumberjacks swelled Big Bay's population to a thousand.

Since then, no more than a few hundred hardy—or hiding—individuals have lived there year-round. Even summer visitors are relatively few: there are just several tiny motels and one small campground. Summer cottages are scattered along the lakeshores, but there are no condominium complexes. Indeed, only a few buildings are taller than one-and-a-half stories.

Spring was a couple of months old, the morning hazy and still, when I packed the car for the trip north to retrieve the kettle. I tried to think like a thief, choosing our less conspicuous car and loading it with what I imagined to be breaking-and-entering supplies: flashlight, screwdrivers (Phillips and flathead), mallet, wrench, crowbar, tote bags, small stepladder, and hand drill. Camps—as second-home cabins are called in Michigan's Upper Peninsula—all around the lake are mostly deserted in May, and I expected the new Tennessean owners wouldn't leave their mild spring weather for Big Bay's rainy season. I was probably going to be able to be as loud and slow as I wanted. Something would give; a window or a door would have been left unlocked. When I was a very small girl, local custom was to leave unoccupied cabins not only unlocked but stocked with emergency supplies once the weather turned snowy, something which regularly happened in October. Someone, a hunter most likely, might seek shelter when a storm pounded down from Canada. Winters were that harsh and unpredictable. Twenty-five years ago, if I had timed things carefully, I could have walked right in.

Frivolous supplies went into a couple of canvas totes. I packed a spade, plastic pails (to transport wildflowers back for our garden), even packing paper (for old juice glasses, a couple of coffee mugs, the idea of which did make me smile), and my old manual camera with the excellent lens. The whole process would have been hilarious if it wasn't so sad.

~

Here is the loss I was inventorying as I packed: three hundred feet of Lake Independence frontage, two rustic cabins with all furnishings—including the kettle, once our source of hot water—two well-tended outhouses, one wooden footbridge over a gully of sweet William, a dock that doubled as swim platform and sundeck, two aluminum skiffs with oars and outboard motors, and a meticulously maintained though oft-repaired ski boat and boat hoist, both of which seemed as old as my parents. All of this was priceless to me still—because of who once lived there, but also because of who I was there. In the cabins, and in the forest, hills, and water that surround them, I was a child rather than a girl, and it was in those wild places that I came to know the rich complexity of the natural world. I could give myself over completely to my imagination. I wandered almost as freely as the French explorers who came before me, giving names to all my special places: Secret Garden, Sand Dune, the Stump.

Christine Rhein

GOOGLING *CHRISTINE RHEIN*

I marvel at all the accomplishments
of my alternate selves: *Christine Rhein,*
Figure Skating Champion of Rockford, Illinois
and *Vice President, Board of Directors,*
State Bank of Mishicot, Wisconsin.
How comforting to know, in other parts
of the Midwest, I've not only learned
how to skate a perfect double axel
but also, finally, to balance
a checkbook, perhaps performing
both feats at the same time.
                                        At the *Turkey Night*
Grand Prix in Las Vegas, *Chris Rhein*—
balding and in need of a shave—
is posed beside a midget race car,
a testosterone-red *Cavalier Connection.*
OK, so I came in 30th (out of 34)
but at least I used *an Ecotec engine*
running on methanol alcohol fuel.
                                        In Germany,
I am *Doktor Rhein* with a paper on *Aortic Root*
Surgery: Comparison of valve-sparing
reimplantation versus composite grafting,
and also *Fitness Leader Rhein* explaining
her Frankfurt program via *Translate this page*:
Because the perseverance range various,
and who already puts the sports badge down
three times has, silver gets, before there is
gold medal starting from the fifth time.

The real me
offers an occasional motion at a meeting
of the *Brighton High School PTA,*
a contribution to the *Friends of the Library,*
some poem titles in journal archives,
and—oh yes, an *honorable mention*
for *Woodpecker,* its short lines,
a crazy Morse code . . .
everyone busy hammering,
busy nodding, as I am at the fitness instructor's
website banner: *The activities are so varied*
that actually for each person
somewhat among the facts
it should be that there is joy.

Christine Rhein

Friday Night

and we're not perched at some neon-lit Manhattan bar,
not dancing in the ballroom of the San Francisco Ritz

but mixing martinis in our Michigan kitchen,
a pot of potatoes on the stove, our twenty-year-old

formica piled with newspapers, bills, sons' projects—
bean plants growing well beyond the experiment.

I think of all the variables affecting a marriage . . .
How lucky to sit at this counter, to watch you

lift the frosted glasses from the freezer, your hips
moving in rhythm as you bounce the deco shaker,

its jangle of gin and ice—and that drop of liqueur
you add, tinting the cocktails robin egg blue.

Judith Calleja

Carolina Sweetgrass

Her serene old hands wrap the sweetgrass strands
around a tightly lashed circle, the base of the form to come.
A strong base she made herself, to build the basket—
to hold the berries, the pine nuts, the warm scented bread.
Her curbside workshop forms an oddly quiet island
where the stream of inattentive tourists break their flow—
one step left, one step right—
pouring along the alternating squares
of deep shade and clear bright sunlight.

Celia asks how long she has used this spot.
A long time, she says. It's the best place,
across from the old churchyard.
Might not be much longer, though.
The grass is hard to find. Have to take a bus
way out to the edge of the city where the sweetgrass still grows.
Maybe soon there'll be no more grass.
Maybe soon there'll be only city.

Don Hewlett

Idle Time

Don Hewlett

Idle Time

I watch her through the branches,
this pleasant looking girl in flour sack dress and bare feet,
walking in the quiet meadow grasses,
selecting Black-eyed Susans and pink Sweet-Williams,
weaving them in a string with daisies and orange Wood Lilies.
When it is long, she circles across the forehead and
entwines it in her copper hair, so both drape to the waist.

She walks holding a bouquet and
with a nodding bow of the head, smiles left then right.
At a wide black boulder she accepts an unseen hand,
that helps her climb onto this stone carriage.
Placing reins in her left hand, the right waves to both sides
and then snaps a whip above the stallions.
A sudden breeze blows at the dress hem and
lifts the flowered hair from her back.

Sandor Slomovits

WHAT IS WAR?

On the way home from school, my daughter asks from the back seat of our car, "Dad, what is war like?"

She loves language and words, and frequently asks for definitions.

"It's when someone, or a group of people, behave in a hostile, threatening way," I reply.

"No dad. I said, what is war. . . like?"

She's eight years old, and when not under the amusing delusion that she knows everything, often still operates under the even more charming one, that her parents do. I resist the temptation to rely on the "war is hell" cliché, and instead say, "You know how sometimes kids get into a fight at school? War is when whole countries get into a fight."

"What do countries fight about?"

"Some of the same kinds of things kids do. One country may have something another one wants, like land, or..."

"You mean like when Simon and Jake both want the tire swing at the same time?"

"Exactly." I know it's not that simple, though it often seems just as childish, but I don't tell her either of those things.

"Why do you ask, honey?" My wife and I, trying to protect her childhood as long as possible, have deliberately shielded her from media news stories about the buildup to war, and have not discussed the events with her.

"One of the kids at school was talking about Iraq and this guy Saddam Hussein. So what is war like?"

Of course, she was bound to hear. And undoubtedly some of the boys, who seem to know as much as the Pentagon about the military machines used in combat, have regaled her with tales of precision guided bombs, F-16s and Tomahawk Cruise Missiles.

But I know that's not what she is asking about.

So, I tell her that I've never fought in a war. That I don't know anything about war first hand. Horrifying images from "Saving Private Ryan" and Kenneth Brannaugh's "Henry the Fifth" rise in my mind. I push them aside, refusing to be frighteningly graphic.

I also decide to say nothing about what her grandparents endured in W.W.II concentration camps. Of my mother who, after escaping a death march from Ravensbrück, survived for weeks on potatoes she dug from abandoned gardens in burned out Dresden. Or of my father's frostbitten toes, the only physical, visible reminder of several bitter Poland winters in a forced labor camp. Of other horrific memories and invisible scars that I know they bear, and ones I'm certain they never told. I push these images aside too. As my parents did with me, I will wait until she is older. And perhaps even then I won't tell her all I've heard.

What I do say, carefully picking my way through the minefield of these images, sounds hollow and unconvincing.

She doesn't buy it.

"Dad, I still don't get it. Can you explain more clearly? Why are we going to war?"

I resist the urge to give voice to my feelings of cynicism, anger, and helplessness. Instead, I tell her, in carefully sanitized language, what President Hussein has done. She seizes on the word *president* and makes a childlike connection.

"Why on earth would the people of Iraq elect someone like that?"

Which leads us onto safer ground, an explanation of various systems of government. I begin by explaining that not all countries elect their presidents and leaders the way we do. And again resist the urge to say something bitter about how we elected our current president. Or about regime change, at home and abroad.

My dry, intellectual narration holds little interest for her. She brings the discussion back on track.

"Dad, what countries have gone to war?"

I tell her the sad truth. And then she comes to the heart of the matter.

"Dad, will you have to go fight in this war?"

"No, honey. Only young people fight in wars." As soon as the words leave my mouth, I desperately wish I could take them back. Both because of their tragic truth and because I instantly know what's coming next.

"Will I have to go to war?" It sounds like she means *now*. She is not quite four feet tall and weighs less than fifty pounds.

"No, honey, you're too young." Like a careless piece on a chess board, I have gotten myself snared in a trap of my own making.

"Will I have to later?" She speaks simply and matter of factly of what I find unspeakable, almost unthinkable.

I reassure her as best I can. I am not satisfied with any of my answers. And I fear I'll have plenty more chances to practice giving better ones. If there are—or ever will be—any better ones.

Larry Francis

When You Die, You Take Your Oldest Face with You—for Mom

Old contains young.
Everyone knows that.
Everything you ever were is in there somewhere, covered
a little more every day of your life.
There are layers of faces underneath the one you die in.
And if you're lucky enough to live a good, long life,
You'll leave a trail of your pictures that could reach the sky.
But the face we say goodbye to goes with you.
And we won't see it again.
And when now we think of you
We get to choose any of the faces you've left behind.

I saw one just a few minutes ago that I'd forgotten.
A picture of you helping me scrape that damn old paint
Some previous resident put on the brick of our house.
That was your 70-year-old "I can still outwork Any Young Person" face:
Very intent and, as usual, very glad to work hard.
Just like the younger version I used to see all the time at the
Statler Hilton
Where you must've hung up 50,000 coats in the most well-
Organized Coat Check Operation in the History of Coat
Checks.
Now your work face was, by nature, related to your "I am
preparing food for a Special Occasion. Please stay out of my way" look
But that look was but a prelude to your "I, too, get to Eat this
Wonderful Food I'm Making" face, a pleasant one indeed
And a face I can't help but note that I seem to have
inherited (except for the part about making the food).
And when Dad carried in the Plum Pudding, all ablaze,
Your face lit up too
Happy amongst other reasons, I suppose,
That the 10 times or so during the year you went to the
downstairs frig
To re-soak the pudding in brandy paid off so magically.

And I can remember the face
I usually only saw in the mirror
When you'd remove your glasses to rub some Ponds cream
On your 100% Irish skin-skin that never needed any make-up.
That was a lovely face.

Or I can see your face in the balcony of St. Matthew's gym
The time that you came with Dad on a school day afternoon
To see your son play in the big 5th grade basketball championship.
We lost about 43–9 but since the whole concept of
    competitive sports wasn't such a live-or-die proposition for you,
You were still proud. Thank you for watching.

But without argument, your finest face, and one of the finest
    Faces humanly possible
Was the look, still visible, in any photo of you with my father.
It's the look of a woman who, without a shred of doubt, knows
    with unswerving certainty that she has found, out of any
    number of clowns who must have come calling on such a Looker
      as you, the Perfect Man to whom she will gladly be
    Attached for life.
If the doubters, and those who Think too Much, would question
    The existence of such a thing as Love...
Well, I've got a few hundred pictures to enter in evidence.
No one did that look as well as you, Mom.

And although I wish I couldn't,
I can see your face when I hurt it.
It was a perfectly composed face, except for the one (and
    only one) tear
Which somehow escaped your control
And reminded me, shamefully, of what a big jerk I had been.

And, if I want, I can see one of your older faces too,
After Mr. Alzheimer came to stay with you.
At the dining table in the nursing home, trying to feed you
grimace which so perfectly
When some other diner would raise a ruckus over something
And you would make a great funny face at me.
Your arched eyebrows and fake
well said, "What the heck's wrong with them?" followed
By one of your good-hearted laughs.
It felt so good to see your old, young self for a moment.
Not even Mr. Alzheimer could cover your mischievous face.
And now I sit here outside a T.J. Maxx, doing a far worse job of controlling
my own tears, writing this
And when I finish, I'll go in and buy the first pair of dress
pants I've bought in 25 years
Because I remember your "He shows up to everything wearing
jeans" look
And I don't want to see that one today.

So, maybe the truth IS that old covers up young
So much so that looking at an old photo of ourselves
We wonder how we've come to look so different.
It seems unkind for age to do such unlovely things
To us
When we were such lovely creatures starting off.
But when you go
The oldest face goes too.
And everything that age covers
Comes out again, in our pictures and our memories,
And that face we said goodbye to yesterday is gone
And any day
We can, to any face of yours we want,
Say Hello.

Esther Hurwitz

WAITING FOR THE TEA TO STEEP

It's three minutes in a morning
that you'll never get back.
You can spend them clearing
the dishwasher or wiping the counters,
but timing is of the essence
because at three minutes and 10 seconds
the brew becomes bitter.
So you surrender to it,
as you give up the rest of the world
when you take your first step into a labyrinth.
Once you start the path there is nothing to do
but watch where to put your foot.
Your only purpose is to get to the middle
and then come back.
At the end, you discover your journey
took you into the deep blue black
of your unconscious, which is located
right behind your right ear.
The tea goes down sweet and hot.

Cristina Trapani-Scott

PHOTO ON THE CELLAR WALL

Sicily must be another world to my
father who grew up in Detroit.
I've seen the all-American photo
of him as a boy on the grassy front lawn
of his parents' home where he's posed
in a white baseball uniform
ready to take a swing.

Another picture, maybe a similar one,
hung once on a cellar wall in Trapani.
I've seen the cellar and the house
where his father grew up, the kitchen
dark and cave-like, the patio cement
worn smooth from his family's feet.
I sat in that house, in the living room
at a long table, dining with his relatives
who spoke the old language around me
as I tried to learn what the walls knew.

I watched faces in the mirror
that stretched along the back wall,
the uncle with my father's round face,
his hair grayer, his
front tooth stuck
to a loose mouthpiece, so that every night
when we parted and he said *a domani*
his tooth danced like a pebble
on his tongue.

My mother told me, as we stood
with the women in the kitchen,
that my father's grandfather kept the picture
on the cellar wall to kiss when he went to retrieve wine
for dinner. I pictured him descending

into the dark cellar, one hand fishing
for the pull switch, the other
brushing the wall searching for the photo,
pausing to feel something beyond
the smooth finish,
to see color in black and white.
then pulling a dusty bottle of wine
from a creaking rack, he'd turn
toward the steps, tug the long
string and return to the world above.

Cristina Trapani-Scott

SEWING PINS AND SALAMANDERS

I look for the words
that fall
from the doctor's lips
and disappear
into crevices
in the cold tile floor.

I gather them, the words
like sewing pins, sharp
and too
thin to get my fingers around.

I throw them into the diaper bag
loose, knowing that each time I
reach in they will prick
my fingers and draw my
blood into them.

Better my blood than hers,
the baby who sleeps in my lap.

Already, I feel her
shape shifting becoming
smaller, thin and sleek like a salamander.

Could she really slip away as fast?

Just another question to drop into
the firefly jar, another hole
to poke into the top
to let it breathe,
and breathe
it will,

until we all are in the jar,
swimming
in the black ink,
trying
to keep the salamander
from slipping away.

Rick Solomon

BURNING OUT

My day begins in the nursery
    where birth is "but a sleep and a forgetting".
It's romantic, in theory: Little bones,
    back from trudging among the stars,
take flesh. Lips to nipple. Breath
    to baby's breath. Star dust
still between his toes.
    And this little piggy's hooked on cocaine
and this little piggy's brain's gone. .

I catch myself singing gospel—
    listening to a little heart, feeling a fontanelle,
running a finger down their spines.
    —"I'm tired of this life I'm living
I'm tired of this world of sin. . ."
    —birth days of the innocents
tucked into the sadness of the world.

My day ends, up here in the tower,
    tenth floor, Allegheny General
in the darkening cave of my office. I'm tired
    of the rotten stench of perfection,
unimpressed by the smashing of atoms,
    the telescoping of stars, the invention of zero.
When I stare out at the dim tenement roofs
    parched with decades of steel mill soot
and the bass of gansta rap rises up from North Avenue,
    I think of Torrie. Pregnant. Killed
in a drive-by shooting in the projects.
    The baby died too. Pigeons flutter
to nests among the tenement eaves.

Above the Life Flight heliport,
beyond Three Rivers Stadium,
    half hidden in the western hills:
a brilliant orange sun sets and flares
    pink and red. The horizon's S-shaped clouds
catch on fire. My face, reflected
    in the window, fades with sunset,
eyes the last to go.

Rick Solomon

CROSSING BORDERS

(for Ray Helfer M.D.)

Ten years ago I came to you
with my first case from the ER. A little boy
left alone overnight in his crib, screamed
until someone called the police.
You said it shouldn't hurt to be a child
but the smell of alcohol and cigarettes on his father's breath,
the emptiness in his mother's crack-ridden eyes,
the never ending blame, hands that hurt,
the taste of blood. . . Every sense
left his body and lived in exile across borders.
Teach him to 'speak sensory', you said.
But I was speechless in a foreign country
where there was too much to feel.
Then, in your quiet way, you taught me
even children with bloodied lips and broken bones
love their parents; that abused abusers
will always hurt their children, recalling
the strap against their back when they were young.
But pain didn't have to be inherited.
And I didn't have to run away from mine.
Last year, I invited you to lecture
about 'Mothers in Captivity' and families without fathers.
At our last meal together, we laughed instead
about *our* fathers holding on to our bicycle seats,
sweating all the way down the street
while we pedaled until we found our balance.
Since then I've hidden a baby in a blanket
so his mother wouldn't bond before adopting him out.
I've seen a teenager, still bleeding from birth, handcuffed
and taken away from her newborn in the name of justice.
I've rocked infants jittery from cocaine withdrawal
every week I've been in the newborn nursery.
And I've examined a three year old girl with no hymen.
Yesterday, when I listened with my stethoscope
to a little boy in the office,

hand to his heart, hand on his back
and heard, in that distance, these sounds of exile,
I kept my balance, crossed the border
from outrage to compassion
to that country between us
again, thanks to you.

Shutta Crum

FATHER'S CUPBOARD

My father's cupboard—built by hand,
held baby food jars and Prince Albert tobacco cans
full of nails or screws.
And always, oily boxes with torn labels
too heavy for me to tip and peek into.
These were the secret things my father used
to hold the world together.

Committed these past fifty years to the basement,
bracing the house I grew up in,
it was once Mom's kitchen cupboard.

Dad painted it smiling-teeth white and Kool-aid red.
It sat near-to-bursting in the kitchen
until banished in favor of Danish modern.

This morning, jacking up the floor above,
it takes four of us to extract the cupboard
from the embrace of defeated joists.
For the house is sagging now,
despite the stoic Danes, despite Dad.

I brush away cobwebs, check all its porcelain knobs.
It is dripped with spilled paint—pink on the red.
Perhaps the pink he used making my own
small table and chairs? Or the pink
of my sister's dollhouse—almost forgotten.
And sky blue. Perhaps a birdhouse,
or a project of my brother's? Maybe it is the blue
of the lone chair that sat in the yard
idly reflecting on the sky, while I attended school,
met boys, and fell in love.

My father's cupboard is scarred and anointed with color.
Until the very end we left it to its labors.
And only now, wrest it from the grieving house.

Shutta Crum

Five Mountain Morning Haiku

1.
Valleys cradle clouds.
Above rise proud peaks, mothers
Of the infant rain.

2.
Quick! Guests are early.
Mountain boasts cloud finery
Flung on his bald head.

3.
Mountains wake grumpy—
Grandfathers with clouded brows.
No loud words today!

4.
Uncle mountains crouch
To leap brightly from cloud beards,
Hoping children laugh.

5.
Rumpled cloud blankets
Slip off mountain's white shoulder.
Wake up, sleepy-head!

Jeff Kass

SONS AND FATHERS

Afternoons, when I return from work
Julius, my fifteen-month-old son
runs to greet me shouting "Dada"
as he claps his hands "Dada"
"Uh uh, burr, burr."

what he means
is I should hoist
him *up* and toss him
in the air so he can fly
like a *bird*

of course, I oblige
for what is more
glorious than the gift
of my son's smile bathing me from above
his hair spreading behind his head
a golden halo

for a brief moment
his teeth shine
in open-mouth wonder
as, perhaps eight inches
of freefall air

eight inches of thrill and fear
exist between his full
bouncy belly
and my careful
waiting fingers

"more, more" he says
as I throw him in the air
ten times, eleven times
before my arms grow tired
and I pull him back down

he leans into me
pats my chest
with his tiny palm
says again, a little
more softly "Dada'"
and I understand who I am

In the morning paper
I read the story of Ishmael
a young father fleeing
from his burning village in Chad
near the border to Darfur

he cradles his own
fifteen-month-old son
as he runs

Janjaweed militia aim machine guns
and chase him on thundering horses

when they catch him they put a bullet
through his brain, taking care first
to yank his son from his arms

What I've noticed when I toss
Julius in the air

is that his shrieks of delight
sound not in the instant he hovers
his hair billowing behind him

then, in fact, his eyes
betray a minute startlement
has my father really done this
he seems to be asking

let me go like this
unfettered, unanchored
in the breeze?

Instead it is when he lands safely
in my hands that he laughs, as if
yes, I've gotten away with it
I've flown free and returned
home unharmed

In grand genocidal tradition
of Nazi Einsatzgrupen
the Janjaweed do not
waste bullets on babies

I wonder when Ishmael's unnamed son
is tossed into the air if he too
offers the look of startlement
of my beautiful boy Julius

have I really been
let go like this
to fly unfettered
unanchored in the breeze

before no one catches
him and he feels a rush
of heat before his skin pops
and burns and his wails
disappear in the bonfire
they make of his body

Mary Jeselnick Koral

Broken Glass (excerpt from *Thicker Than Water*)

After a year's rehab, my daughter comes back home to stay. This is serious coming home, no weekend visit, not a trip to Union. Ken and I are uneasy, who knows if she'll stay put? We want her to *stay put*. Anita says she wants to *stay put*. But two weeks after she comes home to us, she starts taking off again, like her safety lock's broken, and she can't do a thing about it.

Sometimes, when she takes off now, she leaves me a note, sometimes not. Sometimes a phone message, or maybe no phone message, depending. If she leaves any tangible evidence, it's in another language, like atonal—*Gone shopping*.

Which means,

she is or is not having her nails done, painted half moons in blue;

she is or is not buying cigarettes and wine coolers;

or, she might be looking for someone.

Seventeen now, and trouble's friend.

And I keep taking her back, although I'm not supposed to.

Let her experience the consequences of her choices. This is the advice of every person who has ever given us advice. And it's the position that Ken wants to take when he's most frustrated. *Let her go if she wants to go so bad*. He said that while I wept. He sounded hurt and mad that the girl he loves seems to prefer any other place to this place.

I still take her back though; I keep thinking that I'll be able to show how much I love her, then, surely, she'll stay around and lap up some of that love. I always leave the door unlocked when she's gone. I don't want her to be *locked out,* and it's not too hard to convince Ken to go along; I am unable to imagine the worst, no more girl, and he's unable to force me. So, I continue to take her back, and he lets me leave the door unlocked, but he doesn't think it's a good idea, so he only tolerates what I do. He doesn't actually do it himself. That's where we are.

In this place where we are, I consider the evidence my daughter leaves around; there's never any proof whether she means to stay with us or not. All I have is minutia: hair in the sink, a nail paring, the way bed covers are turned back. I hold her picture up to the light and look at her teeth, the turn of her head.

My Calcutta Babe — she's got X written all over her, a love story gone wild. But, she is so sweet. If you fall down in front of her wearing a ratty sweater and no socks, she'll help you up.

Occasionally, she spots a dead grackle or a sparrow while we're driving. Once, she found a red-tailed hawk. When this happens, she yells for me to pull over; she makes a dash, grabs the dead bird, and we drive on. We take it home and have a little burial. It's comforting, the quick turn over of ground, putting the body in, spreading the dirt, stomping it down and walking away.

It is almost pleasant because it's something like ordinary.

And we don't live ordinary.

About a month after she comes home from Wedgewood, we're ready to move. It's moving day to the house on Broadway. There are boxes of her things to be packed yet; the rented truck's in the driveway, and there's no daughter to help. The greenhouse window is still full of those small empty vodka bottles, a few dead plants and her journal. Stuffed animals, clothes, her leather jacket are heaped in a corner of her room.

I know this scene from before; it's the scene where Ken says, *we're going.*

This time, he picks up the jacket and sniffs it like he's a dog hunting clues. Then he drives off, furious. An hour or so later, he finds her walking down Broadway, the street we're moving to. Why is she walking down Broadway? Alone? But, there's no story she's willing to tell. Ken opens the door and tells her to get in. He brings her home to me and hands her over like she's something he's reluctant to move, but I want to, so he will.

He's that mad.

She's mad too, surly with Ken for finding her, maybe, or more likely, surly about the move? She tosses things into boxes and grocery bags, clothes, bottles, makeup, all of it shoved in, spilling out. We haul the mess out to the truck with my daughter in a pick-quarrel mood; I'm quiet. *Move,* I think. *Let's move. I don't want this house anymore.* But, she says I'm way wrong; things aren't going to be better anyplace else. I'm crazy to think so.

At least I won't be here, I think. *At least I won't be in the same place. Someplace different might have a different ending.*

Our first night in the new house, somebody who means business breaks into the old house, smashes the green house window and spray paints her room with a skull and crossbones, fat looped letters that make words I can't read, but surely know the meaning of. We find the mess the next day when we all go back to make a final run through.

"Whoooee," says Anita, the girl who eats red pistachios with my mother. She has to look cool about this, doesn't want to let us know it's what it is, disaster.

Ken turns to her, gets her in a grip, hands on her shoulders, his face right up next to hers. He shakes her, not brain-damage hard, more like he's trying for what reason she might have left in her. Sõn and Jung stare.

"Are you crazy?" he shouts. The sound of *crazy* fills the room.

Crazy, I'm so crazy.,.

"You could get killed! Your brothers could get killed. Your mom, or me. No more, no more. You can't bring us down with you."

It can be hard to pick a worst moment.

But, I finally say it. Ken's already said it, just moments ago, and, now, I say it too. I look at her shoving some broken glass along the floor with the toe of her high top, and I know I love her; I do, but:

No more—No more Anita. No more. You can't come back anymore, baby. You have to go.

That's what I say.

~

She tells me now that she can't believe I said it, *no more. You're out of here, baby.* She was sure I'd always take her back, no matter what. After all, she came back from Wedgewood; in fact, that was the plan all along. *Forever,* I said, *forever.*

But when we took her to Wedgewood it was like taking her to a hospital. It was supposed to work, doing therapy, having practice visits, we'd do all that, the best we could, and we'd get our daughter back.

I struggle to explain myself to Anita when we talk now: Why did I tell her, *no more* right then? Why not sooner, or never?

She doesn't like my answer; she doesn't want to know, even now, how bad it was back then. But I tell her what I saw, not a vision, but there, right there in the flesh. I saw three other people. The reason I said *no more,* was the three other people standing there in the graffiti-lettered room, trying not to step on broken glass.

Suzanne Van Appledorn

Sans Clothes

Alex dresses a capella,
Doesn't much like wearing clothes;
Throws off garments at the door
With little hands and little toes.

Garments are just so restricting,
Painting scenes in blues and reds.
Cleanup's easy; saves on washing
When it's skin instead of threads.

Bathing suits get cold and clammy,
"natural" feels best on skin.
Tanning lines are non-existent,
Even-colored hues blend in.

Cooking-dining make for pleasure
Unconfined by cuffs and sleeves.
Red hot sauces, oily drippings
May require bibs, if you please.

Potty training's very easy
When not wearing underwear.
You can wait as long as poss'ble
When the business end is bare.

Laundry day can be a hassle,
Washing, drying, ironing too.
When no clothes are in the hamper...
Lots of fun things one can do.

Beads and bags and high-heeled shoes,
Accessories are ala mode.
One must be a classy lady
Even though the clothes are stowed.

Someday clothes will be important,
She'll enjoy a shopping spree.
Meanwhile she'll live unrestricted,
Child of nature, garment-free.

Kristin Stelter

TATTOO

At first, he said it in pencil.
Then he wrote it in pen,
followed by colorful tips of markers gripped
tight
          through winters and long nights

As it grew, the edges he drew became
          wings and lions and sunsets.
Until, at last, he was finished.

Now set permanently under her skin,
I love you means so much more
          than it ever could
          with a pencil
          and paper.

Kristin Stelter

THE LETTER I NEVER WROTE

Kristin, what you need to understand is that
God has a plan and I trust him

By the end I couldn't see straight
Trudging through muddy medicated waters
All I could do was eat, sleep and pray
That someday I could spend the whole day with you
But that was just a dream

You only fourteen and I with my cross to bear
Your father overwhelmed and brother so young
I can only blame myself for how I handled things
and for not telling you the truth

Kristin you were there, you just don't remember
11 surgeries
2 ostomies
Radiation
Chemo

At least I kept most of my hair
Though it was thinning

At least I tried all I could to live
Though it nearly killed me

At least I kept most of my pride
Though it dissipated with time

Kristin, this was radical evasive maneuvering
This was every spark of energy I had devoted to living
This was me giving up my body
My mind
My organs
To science
To live
For you and Scott and Dad and God and me

Kristin, I had to shit and piss into bags attached to my stomach
I had to paste them there myself
Wearing diapers to contain the leakage that the doctors
couldn't tell between
Cancer and infection

Can you imagine how it felt?
So disgusted by my relapse ridden scar tissue being
That I wouldn't let your father see me naked

I was sustaining my "normal" life in vain
Flirting with death's uncompromising smile
This loathsome feeling towards my own body
A hopeful laugh disguising messages of *help me*

No one understood what it meant when I said
That I was no longer a woman

They took everything
All I had left was a heart that loved you

I'm sorry that wasn't enough
I'm sorry that I scared you but
Death is supposed to be frightening

And I wasn't ready
How could I be?
Only fifty, I would not go quietly
I know you didn't get the chance to say goodbye
That last day I couldn't speak
I was trying to say I love you
and I'm bitter that I didn't get to know the grown up you

Kristin,
I'm sorry about the cigarette burns on the floor
I'm sorry about my selfish shopping trips
Being a perfectionist, and making you go
    to all those family get-togethers
And to get this out,
I'm sorry for missing every birthday, Thanksgiving,
    and Christmas
I'm sorry for missing your wedding and first and second child
I'm sorry for missing your successes, your triumphs
    and your failures
I'm sorry I can't be there to scratch your back

Don't apologize to me for all the stupid things you did
    —And yes, they were stupid—
I forgive you for them all

Don't worry about me
I'm up here with the Big Guy
Looking down on you
He told me to tell you that he's proud of you
And I am too
Though I must admit, Jesus was pretty mad
    when you denounced him in front of my mother

Kristin keep your chin up
And if you ever want to talk,
I'm in your heart and in your mind's eye
Even if you can't remember
What you imagine is what's important

I am with you always, whether you like it or not

Remember,

I am the flower that blooms in winter,
the fire that warms you

I am the silent surrender of spring,
blazing your goodnights into good mornings

I am the lazy day of summer,
a humid hug around your shoulders
I am the pre-painted fall canvas,
ready to die to live again

Mother Nature cycles unbroken,
I reside within

Remember that I love you always,
Mom

Michael Moriarty

Remembering Our Walk

You seemed distracted.
I bit that apple—found it
paper
        crumpled
                        dry.
Another decision.
We took the route that didn't lead past your old house.
The light
        wet you with its blessing.

And now I wish the updrafts in my head hadn't
                                        swept away
                                                the words we shared.
I wish you were here.
I would dip my dry brush
eyelids in your comfort. I would
stop
trying to remember
                        to mine that moment
                                        for something special
to impress
that verbal
forever.

You were there. That made it.
Miracle. I'm tracing
something monumental. Mankind's
saliva geyser jaws have pursued since the invention
of the leashes—reality and perception.
And here I'm tempted
to reference my hand down my pants—
some image of futility. Faltering. Memory. Truancy.
Kiss Me. Euphony. Where were we...

today
we went for a walk
and I don't have to convince myself it was something special.
An addition to the collection of breaths we've shared.
A parade of cells in your presence. Marching
through my veins and trumpeting a song that echoes so loud
you'll have to excuse my minor confusion as I attempt
to remember
this movement.

Michael Moriarty

Life Art

The space between us is a canvas
pain, sadness, joy and chest plates crack then
paint splashes.
The pull toward one massive puddle
drips from fingertips clasped and
lips drawn to lilt smiles
as an old man shuffles past

but that which exists
must in turn dissipate
and we images have wishes to be lifted and displayed
in the museums of genius, beauty, and fame.

No time to breathe when our legacies
are in the eyes of billions of beholders who are busy
polishing the stoic statues of great men
like Da Vinci, Hemingway and McConaughey.
Their faces nestled on shelves between all our expired
    canned good dreams,
but maybe the lesser of us can rest knowing
we left something here
in the gallery:

For me, maybe some string of words that could unleash
a flurry of bees in the stomach of a young man who had not
    yet spoken,
who would go home buzzing and blow the dust off of his story—
forgetting to fit our specific prerequisites for excellence.

I want the alleys and minds I stumbled through
stained with life art after my final spark and writing's a vital start
but catching a collapsing
father would be a brilliant brush stroke.
I clutch hope
to resonate
through those I leave I behind.

I live to touch lives like dawn sweeping through dull sky and
flood the heavens with a lost mind,
be a sunrise, just one time, in one girls eyes
and knowing I ignited her smile I could retire
to the no-place where skin and consciousness release us.

We want to be masterpieces,
maybe not legends through the ages
but we can all advance together, meet me at the apex
where compassion and greatness stand hand in hand
    and I can hardly take it.
Where it doesn't matter if you wrote eternal plays
or millions of people knew your name
because you generously tipped your waitresses
and cooked, for once, on mother's day.
You brushed tears from loved one's faces
and were always kind to strangers.

This is for every so called
ugly, untalented, unathletic, unable to meet requirements for
pedestal placement person.
Your glory lives in actions—
your imprint cannot be missed in the faces of those you live with.
The mindless grind of nine to five cannot swallow
    your simple friendliness.
Your influence outlasts legend, transcends comprehension—
with eternal echo in every word and movement.
Alive and vibrant
divine enlightened.
The sky is a playground for souls who can't stay down
    and please remember this
human excellence
never fits
until you see yourself
everywhere
on the day when our planets closest star quits
You are a masterpiece because of how you treat your fellow artist.

Laszlo Slomovits

A Way of Choosing

Art is a way we breathe the beauty
of this world into our lives, and how
the necessary grief of living is given

meaning. It is a sweet way of choosing
awareness—the heart kind, with its grace.
Otherwise we just chew the charms of life

without ever tasting them. Come. Let's
not be strangers to our own loveliness.
Let not even one of us be left out of this

choosing. Let's journey from one welcome
home to yet another welcome home.
Let beauty be the road, the way we move,

where we come from and where we go.
And let us breathe deeply, together,
this beauty-suffused life.

Laszlo Slomovits

Any Time

Unlike in fields—subject to seasons—in a human life,
planting, growing, harvesting can occur any time.
The fruit of such living can ripen in Spring
or Winter, and seed can take root any time.

There is nothing hidden in the above four lines
that we can't find in our own life any time.
Age does not regulate seasons for this kind
of farming, though it may decide seed and fruit.

Any time a new start is imagined, felt,
or just deeply hoped for, a newly created sun
rises and quickens the seeds, and rain clouds
start to form above the prayers of well-wishers.

And if we've forgotten or never learned
the proper prayer to bless the crops,
let's make one up. And tomorrow,
another one. Actually, any time. Now.

Kawita Kandpal

What Becomes of a Grace

from the poem "How We Met The Barbarians" from Carl Phillips

Never mind the natural world that restores the lily blossom
above the water table.

Her desire was to name each desire: Sappho,
how many petals have ebbed from your East Aegean?

I have come to be beguiled by your lyric, come
dusk I will lie near your sash of blood orange.

When beauty comes to abandon
the line I will not pause

upon the veil of petals, water, wish: such graces, I place them here.
Say *breath.* Say *become.* Say *this body is beneath the ruin.*

I am leaving a space for your reliquary.

I have memorized the song inside your hand, the nightingales that emerged
from the ghazal, and how once we entered

the arc of their departure.
Is there such an entrance within the blossom
that allows for flesh to withhold the memory of saints?

The feather claims a longer sojourn than the flesh
that collapses around it; consider the quill

And the hand that shores the wound closed. I have loved a woman

longer than—I will have my proof of the infinite,

your hand
            is signature enough for what passes into twilight.

When the day should diminish, I will come for you
            at the closing. I offer my mouth

in exchange for a thousand summers. What else to surrender
            to the narrative abandoned by *now*?

Veronica Sanitate

Barcelona

I feel as sheer today as I did in Barcelona,
that hot day we walked to the ocean and lunched
at a restaurant that belched American music
and cigarette smoke and afterwards I had
a sick headache and retched three times. I should've
recognized it coming on—feeling as removed
and costumed as the mimes on Las Ramblas who
would shut down and fold up their complicated lives
reviving only to the clink of Euros in their baskets.

Back at our cardboard hotel at the edge of the city,
I drank Pedialyte and slept fitfully through the dinner
everyone agreed was the worst of the trip. I readied
myself for the evening; the Flamenco couldn't be missed.
I dressed in black—sexy, you said—and we boarded
the bus. Somehow, I had recovered, or had reversed,
or like a mime, revived myself, morphing together
two lives, each painted-over and slightly revised. Someone
took our picture; I was holding your arm, dearer than
you could've imagined, because I was so sheer. Only
partially in my body; the rest of me an apparition
drifting back to the heat on a bench in the city, looking,
even with eyes half-closed, at the magnificent buildings,
the ornate rails on the balconies, the trees on the Rambla
de Catalunya—too huge for acacia or magnolia—shading
me while I slumped there nearly green, Mary keeping guard
and writing half a dozen postcards on my left; an autistic
savant to my right rocking as he scanned a small-print
tract with thin-lined graphs and math, while you walked
to see Gaudi's Casa Batlló, astonished, I imagined,
at the façade that seemed to undulate in fantastical
waves much the same as I felt, swelling and swaying
just before sickness, though later you said I hadn't
missed much. Perhaps my dream the night before,
waking suddenly with a gasp as I watched my death
a century ago as a young Spanish man...

Now, as I gather my self to dine with the friends
with whom we toured Barcelona, I feel sick again.
But I rally in time. I dress in dark silk and earrings
that sparkle, transparent only to those who can notice.
Illness serves us by showing us. A moon illumines
the path—its sheer gold revamps the black. And I
take your arm again tonight, tourist on this continent,
shimmering between the worlds.

Sandor Slomovits

WHAT ELSE CAN WE DO?

Two weeks after the events of September 11, I finally told my seven-year-old daughter what happened that day. My wife and I had made a deliberate decision in the days following the tragedy to shield our child from the news, especially the horror-filled TV images.

But now it was time. If we did not tell her, she would hear about it from someone else. So in the car, after school, on our way to an event where I knew it was likely to come up, I told Emily. Briefly, with a minimum of graphic details, but leaving nothing out.

It is a natural urge all parents have, to protect their children from terrifying images and frightening stories; to wait as long as possible to expose them to the sometimes cruel, unbearably sad realities of our world.

I was sixteen when my mother first told me that she was my father's second wife. That he'd lost his first wife and three children in Auschwitz twenty-one years earlier. That she'd lost her only brother and her fiancé. I had few questions for my mother that day. The information she gave me was too vast, too incomprehensible. She and I rarely talked about it again and more than thirty years would go by before I was finally able to talk with my father about his losses.

Now, in the car, Emily also asked only a few questions. "How far is New York? When did this happen?

We were driving east on Stadium Boulevard and I began pointing out the many American flags and the God Bless America signs and told Emily that these were some of the ways that people were trying to express their support for our country and for the people who lost their friends and relatives. When we stopped for a red light at the corner of Stadium and Packard, we saw members of the Ann Arbor Fire Department at the intersection, collecting donations. I waved one of them over to our car and emptied my wallet into the tall boot he held out. After the light changed and I drove away, I told Emily about the firefighters in New York and how the money I gave would help their families. She said, "Dad, what can I do?" I was touched and relieved. There was no fear in her question, no helplessness. We brainstormed. She too would make a God Bless America and she'd empty her piggy bank.

Then she said, "Dad, what else can we do?" I suggested we could be kind to everyone we met. She enthusiastically amplified. "We could help people. Like if someone falls, we could help them up. Or if someone is lost, we could show them where to go?"

"Yes," I said. "Those would be very good things to do." Over the course of the day she kept bringing up the subject and continued asking, "Dad, what else can we do?"

She didn't ask me about forgiving and I was relieved. It was two days before the Jewish holiday of Yom Kippur. In Judaism it is customary on Yom Kippur to ask for forgiveness for any harm we may have done, and to forgive those who have harmed us. But, for me, right now, it felt too soon to forgive.

I thought of my parents. What did they do on Yom Kippur after they discovered what the Nazis had done to their families? Did they forgive? Later that day I called and asked them, first about the hijackers. Did we need to forgive them on Yom Kippur?

"No," my father said. "If someone comes to kill you, it is your duty to try to kill them first."

Which was the most poetic justification for violence I'd ever heard, but not really a reply to my question, so I pressed on. Had he ever forgiven the Nazis on any Yom Kippur in the last fifty years?

"No," my father said. "Forgiveness does not apply to situations like that." My mother was silent.

Besides his first wife and children, my father also lost both his parents, his only brother and three of his eight sisters in Auschwitz. Perhaps he was right. Maybe forgiveness does not apply to situations like that. Nor to the events of September 11.

Emily asked me why it was the firemen who were collecting donations. I told her of the New York City firemen, and of all the other people, who performed brave, kind and loving actions on that day and since. People who tried, and did, save lives, sometimes at the cost of their own.

I thought again of my parents, how they and others in their families survived, while so many others were destroyed. How they were saved through the grace of God, their own personal strength and the kindness of strangers who helped them, often at the risk of their own lives.

I will not desecrate the memories of the victims of either the Holocaust or of September 11 by comparing them. Yet I will remember, about both events, the generosity and the selfless sacrifice of strangers. I think of the words of Anne Frank. "It's a wonder I haven't abandoned all my ideals, they seem so absurd and impractical. Yet I cling to them because I still believe, in spite of everything, that people are truly good at heart."

And I think often of Emily's question. "What else can we do?"

Robert Fanning

HAPPINESS

Happiness, that fatted calf, hangs
from the ceiling by a thread. Silly-eyed
and frilly, the piñata teases, swaying
like a plump ballerina above the birthday
party guests. When the blindfold goes on,
when laughter and light disappear,

I'm told to thrash the high darkness
until I hit it. Look at me: the village idiot
shaking my fist at the night sky, taking
jabs at its flank, hoping to stab the elusive
cloud, to start a shimmering candy river
for all the thirsty villagers below.

I know they watch from behind the windows
of their dark homes, dreaming the red gold rain.
We each want a taste of it, thirst for it, want it
to fall in our hair, to bounce from our palms,
to get on our knees and thrust our fists
into its shattered rainbow shards.

We won't stop until the last sun-flaked drop
spills, until every piece of joy's flash flood
is gone. And when it's done, when we're all
singing over short candles, slurping blood-red juice
from our thumbs, playing with our new toys—
after the lucky kid fishes one last piece

from the sea of wrappers, we'll be sure
not to look *up*—where that gutted cardboard carcass
arcs like a hung God, dragging like a sharp
pendulum over our heads, a drained slab on a hook,
a reminder of the dry season, of need and loss
and the empty hours we've all long forgotten.

Robert Fanning

Crooked Wisdom

Having learned last night of his wife's affair,
my dentist holds a giant silver spear
and leans over the canyon of my open jaw.
Diving in again, vulture-sure, he picks

at my gum's weak pink flesh. Between
cliffs, down in the bone and coral landscape
of my teeth, nerve tips burst and bloom
like crimson flowers on a hill. Soon

blood's smeared red signature runs
from a deep root and floods my tongue.
Half-under with gas and lovely numb,
I watch his left eye become a clouded moon,

then one black branch of an eyelash
catch a teardrop's sheer balloon. With quick
shame, like a lion tamer stricken with naked
fear, he leaves the work of the open mouth

and the raw wound to another. He lays
the mirror down beside the spear, and exits
the room. Anesthesia doesn't dim his grief
a room away. I hear the hygienist say:

She's leaving you for him. You've seen this
coming for a year...

A bit later he returns, composed in his white
smock, and clips the X-rays of my teeth
to the board. Then he lifts his pointer
to the slideshow of my bite: backlit, exposed,

the skull's little ornaments hang; bicuspids
and molars glow with hunger and decay. *See here—*
he points—*here's the abscess. Here's the cavity,*
and here's that crooked wisdom pushing through.

Jeff Kass

The Naked Ear Is Pink

half a skin-donut
the hole in the middle
not precisely the middle
and not precisely a hole
but a one-way tunnel that smacks
into the dead-end of a drum
what goes in stays in
scuttles around and pounds
against the drum's thin veil
a miner's pick-axe, hungry

what is the lobe
but a swingset for dust
a rest-stop for insects
its pillow belly the underside
of a softly boiled yolk
how does the spiral of the ear
learn to look like a seashell
cut in half
how does the top ridge crisp
like burned bread crust
what mental earthquake
causes the eruption of wax
to flow slow from the ear's volcanic cone

how grow these flesh-flaps
from the sides of our heads
hole first
then the surrounding closets
then the rolled-over
pant cuffs?

Kawita Kandpal

Flesh for my Name

When you come for my name, and the night
    bird upon my tongue, divine the couplet's desire,

Rouse me toward indigo groves with a hundred ghazals. Won't you
    console the form that was woman and once?

Brad Tompkins

Flaming Firetruck

flaming firetruck engulfed in mange—orange-red flames
crimson paint bubbles, yellow stripes blister and
disappear under wavering heat—what should we do?

and yet the fire swaddled truck is not consumed or reduced,
a heat blanket of flames merely undulates up and
down like yellowed lace, above and below—hope set aflame.

a doomlet of fear and ferocity wrapped in orange chiffon
grips the heart, a red sled wreathed in flickering
phantoms, hobbled defenseless—some deemed tragic.

that which we need protection from torments and mocks us,
slips up beside us and makes our most prized defense
another Maginot, another loopy plan gone awry—flaming hate.

this maroon vehicle meant to protect set alight strands us, pride
and faith consumed further hollows our fragile selves,
heads lead pipe struck—who will save us when the saviors fail us?

Brad Tompkins

A Gripe

I have a gripe with the thirteen striped ground squirrels
that have degraded my yard and tunneled and mazed
their insistent way throughout its damaged carpet,
rising soldier straight and victorious on their dirt mounds
to mock as I cane my way across my tunnel mined
dirt scape, leaning like a backyard Pisa whenever
my cane or a brace-encased leg punches though the
dirt-scarred lattice crisscrossing my scraggly sun-fried lawn.

as much as I love nature and God's creatures, these sleek
rodents disturb and pain me, and the memory of my son
Joel blasting one square in the head with lead from a
cheap pellet gun the first time he fired it pleases and does
not disturb me, but now that son has moved on to other
pursuits and these hole-digging machines no longer have to
fear air-powered death (though it seems for every pellet-stilled
squirrel heart, ten rose to replace it and help replenish the dirt maze)

pseudo sages have proclaimed that no person ever really owns land,
land is only rented or borrowed or temporarily possessed, the point
is, I would like to feel, if only fleetingly, that I do possess my near
acre and a quarter for now and do not share it with striped fur-bearing
tunnelers, but only with winged wonders—demure cinnamon sparrows,
tree-trunk-hopping blue gray nuthatches, black-hatted chickadees,
goldfinches flitting in flashing turns and counter-turns, pensive crimson
cardinals, Renaissance colored waxwings diving among the locust leaves.

Chris Moriarty

Come Summer

Come sleeping on summer days that always end too early
Come and whisper into my ear
Come hold my head and finger my hair
Come absence of mind
Come Simpsons' re-runs
Come sleeveless T-shirts and hoops with no nets
Come family dinners
Come hanging out with friends
Come jokes with no punch lines
Come making fun of communism
Come wishing I had more friends
Come kisses on my forehead
Come days that feel like vague dreams
Come poems that I will never finish
Come garden that mom works too hard for
Come sweet lullabies of distant crickets who should be paid
for what they do
Come the dank air of evaporated rain
Come camping
Come hunger for something new
Come art fair
Come loneliness
Come walks to the bakery
Come evoke my madness
Come Monday night breezes through open windows
with chipped paint
Come eat away at me
Come mowing the lawn
Come the relativity of everything in life
Come sitting on a bedroom floor and letting the echo of yourself
ring like broken church bells

Don Hewlett

SOUL

They slowly cruise by with…
the sweet rumble of...
straight pipes.
Engine's power music,
a beat, that sinks
to this street teen's soul.
Hot Rods with…
lowered chassis.
And the cowling,
the cowling removed to show,
gleaming chromed air filters,
between two shining heads.
The body with candy apple
red reflections through six coats of
hand massaged lacquer.
From the mirror
two fuzzy dice, swing,
All this on white tires...
turning, without fenders.
And the girls,
the girls hang on the drivers,
the girls with long bare legs in white shorts,
tops with a button open
displaying the gleaming silver necklaces.
Candy apple red lips, six layers deep,
emitting
soft sweet voices
that sink
to this street...
                    teen's...
                              soul.

Don Hewlett

Sweetwaters Coffee & Tea

Chris Lord

Once Upon Ann Arbor

Ann Arbor, art fairs, Krazy Jim's Blimpy Burger,
basketball at Chrysler Arena, eighty Democrats
eating at Arbor Brewing with one Republican,
and two Libertarians, while ten Greens dance
in the streets with the mayor who is planting
windmills in landfills, switching on LED street-
lights, single-handedly solar paneling City Hall.
Fairy doors appear mysteriously at popular
establishments each morning, notes and pennies
left on miniature porches by Townies on the way
to the Top of the Park, the Power Center,
the Performance Network, gay rights and partner
benefit demonstrations, the painted rock on Hill,
Impeach Bush signs, Iraq, protesters protesting,
Peaceable Kingdom, peaceniks parading until
candles burn their hands, 16 Hands, chocolate
hearts at Kilwin's and chocolate footballs
at the Schakolad factory, Go Blue Saturdays,
Seva's vegetarian cuisine, Long John Silver
and the Kentucky Colonel drinking Starbucks,
Writers Reading at Sweetwaters, Espresso
Royale Caffés, Shaman Drum, Nicola's Books,
unsquared award-winning poets performing
with Patricia Smith at the Neutral Zone,
the student whose porch couch is catching fire,
the student passed up and out in the bleachers,
the student passed up for financial aid,
students at U of M, EMU, WCC. University
salaries, University Hospital, the science and
stem cells that will give some of us extra time.
And God's mistake, the plane that went down in
Lake Michigan with the gifted transplant team.

Washtenaw Dairy donuts, Zingerman's
Downtown, Zingerman's Next Door, and
Zingerman's Roadhouse serving $4 cafs and $2
cookies from a tin trailer on the old West Side.

A man in dirty clothes and a dirt-lined face
picks up a discarded brownie, wipes off the ants.
I follow him downtown, one foot drags, his walk
tripping memory. We pass the Delonis Center,
built with liberal dollars to serve the homeless.
He does not go in, turns and asks if I have any
spare change, and the shivering young woman
sitting on the bench behind him asks if I can
bring her a blanket, says she is cold, always cold.
Says she used to wear a floor-length mink coat
until PETA's petters sprayed her with fleas.

The man frowns, scratches his arms, his scalp,
moves toward Farmer's Market in Kerrytown,
its stalls now bare, no one to ask for money.
A policewoman pulls up beside him. He says
he will find a new door for the night,
no, he doesn't like shelters, they aren't safe.
I look closer. Is he the boy I once knew,
who craved chocolate then heroin, peddled
marijuana to parents after dark on the Diag,
took policemen on a wild motorcycle chase
on neighborhood streets one afternoon,
and spent the night in jail. He was fed well,
he said. He entered rehab. A year later I heard
he was still clean. But one night trouble threw him
from a bike into Ann Arbor's Michigan basement
where he found the old euphoria and the needle
stayed in his arm. He ate trashed greasy triples
at Blimpy Burger, dog donuts at Washtenaw Dairy,
giant shrimp given him by the sympathetic manager
at Long John Silver's, placed a penny for luck
on the Fairy Door at the library where the staff
let him sleep if he held a book and didn't snore.

I see him looking in Schakolad's at a hollow
chocolate house, its roof of cocoa butter shingles,
its raspberry floor. He points at a mint clock,
a set of bitter handcuffs, a sweet motorcycle.
He is that boy I once knew. He says he wants
to spend the night in the chocolate house's door.
Says his DNA is dysfunctional, asks if I have $5.
I give him $10, he asks if he can buy me a drink.
I say no, tell him I'm already high, for I've been
luckier than he in this fair city, rated one
of the five best places in America to live.
I've eaten its frosted windows, opened its ding-
dong doors, swept cold from its raspberry floors.
I've learned the ABCs of Ann Arbor, donated
and deducted bikes, blankets, business casuals,
leftovers from Eve, stepped over homeless Zs
in West Park, crossed streets to avoid looking
in the eyes of the person limping toward me,
asked myself who it is I am afraid to see.

Don Hewlett

Another Day

Esther Hurwitz

Retail Space for Lease

Today it starts somewhere in summer with the wind blowing out
the heat and the sun at its highest.
They've put up a "Retail space for lease" sign
in the storefront window that's been a pinball arcade,
under different owners, for 25 years.
Twenty years ago, I was assistant manager there
and in the silence
and the heat we waited for the sun to start moving again.
The only life was inside the arcade,
inside the machines, where the players slapped at the sides,
gyrated with their hips, keeping the ball in play
through sheer concentration—meditation
feeling the bumps and the slides of the steel ball
in the polished grooves of slick wood.

We'd been listening to Ricky Lee all winter and were waiting
for the other shoe to drop in the dead heat, and the freshest sounds
were Joni Mitchell's "Mingus," not because it was jazz, but because
the sparseness of the guitar, bass, and horns sounded like cool
rain and we were thirsty. And I was having a normal life for a change,
even though I was dating Ed. But he did good the night
he brought just-picked strawberries so sweet
it was like eating them for the first time.

We had a "Playboy" under the counter, but only an anniversary
edition and only because it had stories by great contemporary writers.
You can ask Grandma about it—she asked and we told her.
We never wondered why John, the handsome kid, willingly worked
Friday nights until a year later when we found out he'd sold drugs
out the back door. And the summer dragged on
while I hired a friend of a friend who broke the key off in the alarm
one night at 2 a.m. At least he called to report it; we were up anyway.

We never foresaw anything in the reflections of the glass
    on the machines,
even after wiping them down each night, and gazing
into distorted pictures of sex and coin.
And then it was autumn and I cherished the stillness
of football Saturdays when everyone else was at the game and
the solid state machines shattered the silence, sporadically,
with their attention-getting tunes.

I was last there six years ago with Cousin Marni
    and we left three free games,
driven out by the continuous blasts from the Van Halen machine.
It kept ruining whatever concentration we could muster
despite the flashing backglass, as we tried to guide
that silver ball through too many moving targets.
That machine was all action, alright, but no rhythm, no soul, no chi.

Today the sign flips and flails in the breeze and I have to wonder
what they will put in that space next. What more could they need
on that corner when already it's got used records, five restaurants,
liquor, two pizza joints, and a coffee bar?
I don't know what kids do these days to feel like we did then,
but I do know that if you stand firmly on your own two feet
and hold your arms out perpendicular to your body,
the music rises up out of the floor and takes care of the rest.

Rick Solomon

Ode to Zingerman's Pulled Pork Sandwich

Ah The Joys of Pork, circumcision notwithstanding;
Our inheritance of dread from Adam notwithstanding;
I sit alone in post-prandial bliss in Zingerman's Roadhouse.
(Whoever is not guilty—complicit in his or her comfort
Of daily immoral acts in these end times—cast the first stone.
Even Nestle's (". . . the very best chaw-clate") beans
Are harvested by child slaves in Ivory Coast.) But,
Postmodern in its social responsibility toward fine eating
    (accept killing)
12-dollar-mac-and-cheese-Zingerman's Roadhouse with their
philosophy
Of excellence at any cost has won me over—
At some expense. Oy! They roast the whole pig slowly, slowly,
Slowly on a spit, on site in a big roaster. Then, do they soak it
    (no one knows)
In special juices of papaya, peppers, cardamom and clove
Such as to make the un-embodied angels weep from jealousy?
The west wind's aroma wafts among the strip malls
Up and down Stadium, past the Yoga Center and
The Castle beer, wine, and cigar store and Nicola's bookstore
Pulled muscle, I say, stripped from the bone
Of some smart oinker raised to die for our (double) chins.
And in full awareness of my sins I confess
(With two Coont Ales having passed through the splanchnics
Now soaking my frontal brain with froth)
This is the best foinkin' pulled pork sandwich
In the best big-assed pork soaked sesame seed Kaiser roll
With the best ministered-with-mayo-anointed-in-apple-cider-vinegar-
&-shrived-in-yellow-mustard coleslaw
Exactly matched to the savory tang of pulled pork such that
If the Buddha ate meat he'd eat Zingerman's pulled pork sandwich.

How much of our day is spent in longing
Expecting, anticipating, measuring, waiting for
Our desire to match our expectations? Better even than
the first drag on a Camel after months of failed abstinence
This sandwich fit sire in sow. More than just a met desire,
This alchemy was like some Gnostic recipe for seeing G-d and
I dwelled in Thy House as I savored and sucked swine
With my eyes closed meditating; and chewed it to an essence
And pouched it in my cheek like the strike of a slow curve ball
In the catcher's mitt that ends the World Series
Played over and over again and again in slow motion
And recorded at home on DVD for posterity forever and ever.

Carol Bone

Remember Ann Arbor

I want to remember what I shouldn't forget
Over forty years have gone by since first we met
I came to Ann Arbor in '64
I found it a place to live and do more.
What a place to be in those great times
Great friends, great jobs, and five dollar fines.
I worked the late shift back in the sixties,
Walked past the protests, the take-overs, the hippies.
On the way to the hospital I knew how to learn
On the wards, in the labs, and from the interns.
Back then the hospital was like a family
Afternoon shifts made us closer- them and me.
Old Main had elevator operators who loved to talk
Real people, no computers, nice to ride and not walk.
Mr. Flood's Party was the place to go when work was done
So were Bimbos and The Pretzel Bell-all places to have fun.
When the bell rang and my name was called, I stood on a table
I turned twenty-one and drank all that I was able.
Just some fun in a serious world with serious things
Our lives were just starting, with new experiences to bring
Vietnam, the draft, JFK, and Kent State
Free speech, free sex, free to think, free to mate
The first place I lived was at Madison and Division.
The bathroom shower looked down over Blimpies!
We were all in school and then we graduated
Friends moved away; living alone is over-rated.
The seventies came and I loved to ski
I left Ann Arbor for Aspen; to have fun and be me.
I left for seven years and then returned to A2
I now had a family with a son, Jeff, and a husband too.
I returned to the same job, working evenings again.
Mike was born at Women's; a great life to plan.
Ann Arbor has made my life first rate
Art fairs, Stanger's, football, and tailgates
The nineties brought retirement and a new career
I was finally able to teach; it was easy-no fear

I loved my new life at WCC
And Don and Chris with Sweetwater's poetry
The millennium had brought more good things to me
    Now in 2007, it was time to leave A2
    Florida was the place to start anew
    I am adjusting to the animals, the beach, the heat
    The gators, the birds, the golf are all neat.
Ann Arbor will always have a place in my heart
It is part of my being; where I got my start
I have heard it many times; the sound rings true
Even in Florida we hear Go Blue!!

Sandor Slomovits

Ode to Zingerman's Deli
(A Song)

Let's go get a sandwich at the Deli
I'm sick and tired of peanut butter and jelly
Something really good to fill my belly
Let's go get a sandwich at the Deli

Cream cheese, Swiss cheese, muenster and Dutch gouda.
Where else have you seen so much good fooda?
Bagels, pumpernickle, onion rolls and rye,
Could go elsewhere... can't imagine why.

Let's go get a sandwich at the Deli
I'm sick and tired of peanut butter and jelly
Something really good to fill my belly
Let's go get a sandwich at the Deli

Pesto, tomato and fresh mozzarella
Grill it on rye, make me a happy fella.
Blintzes, latkes, hot potato knishes
We won't even have to do the dishes!

Chris Lord

Ode to Matchmaking at Sweetwaters Coffee & Tea—Au lait! Au lait!

To her, he was a bold untamed sweetheart with a kick,
a gray centaur drinking passion from a blended cup,
stirring dollops of savory memories with his tongue.
She was captivated, watched for an outpouring of woo,
a nod back to a black mythical time when man and horse
perked as one fiery full-bodied brew. At first, she feared
he would jolt and whip her away to an island without
a café; but then she saw he was not a frothy mix—no,
he was herbal and wise, an unbridled fair-trade centaur,
a dearest Darjeeling, a high-steepin' earl, an organic
indulging in sweet caramel mocha, offering carrot cake.

She stepped over sweet water, neighed across the floor,
sampled dragon eyes, monkey caps, gunpowder tea,
eggnog lattes, chocolate-covered sunflower seeds.
She repaired his racing heart, stroked his thinning mane,
said, "Hey, Centa, you half and half hybrid, you're hot!"
He reared, red-eyed, said "Whoa! I'm no double shot—
I'm a single animated caffeinated here and to-go Joe,
lookin' to kick back my hooves with someone who
grasps my bushy tale of woe. " He was flanked by
her first flush of warmth, asked her to linger with him
over Sweetwaters' heady scent of ardor in Ann Arbor.

They wrapped themselves in lemon peel, cinnamon,
jasmine, mandarin orange; honeyed a cherry scone—
stirred steamy stories and poems in intense espresso—
sugar cubes floated toward them on clouds of cream.

Don Hewlett

A Sweet Read

Notes from our Contributors

Zachary Benjamin Baker (pages 16, 17) is the son of Gary and Debby Baker, a huge fan of Dylan Thomas, and a proud member of the Washtenaw Community College Poetry Club. He has been published in *The Huron River Review* and *Blood Orange*. He wishes peace for all; and that each may dream to bring about brighter tomorrows, but live as if they will never need tomorrow. Zachary looks forward to each third Tuesday of the month at Sweetwaters, for Writers Reading.

Scott Beal (page 20) is a poet and educator who lives and works in Ann Arbor. His poems have appeared in journals, anthologies, and his chapbook, *Two Shakespearean Madwomen Vs. The Detroit Red Wings*. He holds an MFA in Creative Writing from the University of Michigan.

Carol Bone (page 118) has written poetry for friends for many years. She has been a high school and college instructor in the Ann Arbor/ Ypsilanti, Michigan area. She hopes to spend more time writing now that she is living in Florida. Her poetry has been published in a Kodak company newsletter.

Sue Budin (page 38, 39) has published poetry in several literary journals including *Ibbetson Street Press* and *Millenium Anthology of Contemporary Poetry*. She was the second place winner in the *Current Magazine* fiction and poetry contest several years ago. She has reviewed poetry for a library journal and has also led writing workshops for youth in her work as a librarian at the Ann Arbor District Library.

Judith Calleja (page 51) is an anthropologist by trade and a sometime poet by inclination. She has been fortunate enough to be published in several journals including the *Wayne Review* and the *Classical Outlook*. Once a lifelong resident of suburban Detroit she is now happily settling in along the Fox River west of Chicago.

Marilyn E. Churchill (page 24) has worked as a bookseller and a college instructor. Her writing has been published in several literary journals including *The University of Windsor Review* and the *Ann Arbor Review*, and in *From the Ground Up*, a publication of the Ecology Center of Ann Arbor. Marilyn has won poetry and fiction prizes in *Current Magazine's Poetry and Fiction Contest*.

Shutta Crum (pages 70, 71) is an award-winning writer of books for children and poetry for adults, as well as a storyteller and a retired librarian. The author of eight picture books and one novel, as well as three forthcoming books, Shutta's poetry has been published in many literary journals. Her articles about writing have been published in several teaching and writing magazines. In 2005, she was honored by being one of eight authors invited to read at the White House Easter Egg Roll.

Lonnie Hull DuPont (pages 4, 5) is an award-winning poet whose work is widely published. She returned to her Michigan roots after living sixteen years away in Greece, New York City, and San Francisco. After she and her husband moved into a pre-Civil War farmhouse on the oldest road in Michigan, she began writing a collection of poems about a fictitious woman living in the house. These poems are from that collection.

Katherine Edgren (pages 14, 15) is a social worker who lives in Dexter, Michigan and works for University Health Service. She received a first place award for the *Writer's Digest* non-rhyming poetry contest and her poetry appeared in *The Year's Best Writing* in 2005. She also received third place in the *Current* contest in 2005. Kathy has been published in various journals including the *Birmingham Poetry Review, Barbaric Yawp,* and *Main Channel Voices,* as well as the *Christian Science Monitor.*

Robert Fanning (pages 100, 101) is the author of *The Seed Thieves* (Marick Press, 2006). His poems have appeared in *Poetry, Ploughshares, The Atlanta Review, and Shenandoah,* and many other journals. A graduate of the University of Michigan and Sarah Lawrence College, Fanning's awards include a Creative Artist Grant, the Inkwell Poetry Award, and the Foley Poetry Award. A Pushcart Prize nominee, he was recently a finalist for the Glasgow Prize for Emerging Writers. His second collection, *American Prophet,* is forthcoming in 2008. His website is www.robertfanning.com

Larry Francis (page 58) has taught high school English for thirty years and enjoyed himself immensely. He has run many student poetry shows, participated in National Poetry Slams as a poet and a quasi-administrator (emphasis on the quasi), and helped run the Ann Arbor Poetry Slam since 1991.

Peggy Gray (page 30) is an artist, poet, and short story writer. Her paintings and poetry have appeared in several magazines, including *The MacGuffin, The Michigan Hibernian,* and *The Irish Connection*. Peggy is a clogger and bodhron player. She is married, has five children and five grandchildren. Peggy has written a country song that one day may be sung on the Grand Ole Opry.

Don Hewlett (pages 53, 107) has published poetry in the *Wayne Literary Review, Poetry in Performance,* and the *Poetry Tribe Review Anthology*. He had a play in the 2004 12-hour play marathon held at Oakland University and a staged reading at the Village Players Theater in Birmingham, Michigan. Don's art has appeared in the *MacGuffin Literary Magazine,* and on the covers of *Bear River Writers Respond to War* and *Field Guide to Luck*. Five of Don's sketches (pages 1, 27, 52, 113, 122) are in this issue.

Esther Hurwitz (pages 2, 61, 114) has appeared on public radio, and was once voted "Ms. Under Appreciated" at a regional poetry slam. Her poems have appeared in many places. *Soft as a Beagle's Ears* is her first collection of poems (www.thewordsmithpress.com). Esther is a freelance writer and editor, and writes the "Toolbox" column for Washtenaw Community College's *CareerFocus* magazine. She is her mother's favorite poet, but her father favored Shakespeare. Esther is co-host of Writers Reading at Sweetwaters.

Kawita Kandpal (pages 92, 103) is a graduate of the Creative Writing Program at Bowling Green State University and lives in Detroit. Her poems have appeared in such journals as *TriQuarterly* and *Puerto del Sol*. Kandpal's book, *Folding a River,* is an exploration of East-West cultures. In it, Kandpal's lingual and cartographic explorations of these cultural landscapes takes her into an emo-mythic place not to be found on any map.

Jeff Kass (pages 72, 102) writes prize-winning poetry, fiction, and non-fiction. His work is published in literary reviews, magazines, and newspapers. He teaches high school English and Creative Writing and is Poet-in-Residence for Ann Arbor Public Schools. In April of 2007, Jeff was recognized by the ACLU as Michigan's Teacher of the Year and was also selected the 2007 Michigan Youth Art's Festival's Artist-in-Residence. Jeff directs the Creative Writing Program at Ann Arbor's Teen Center, The Neutral Zone.

(Jeff Kass, continued.) Jeff has been the Ann Arbor Grand Slam Poetry Champion and the runner-up for 2006 Best Poet of Washtenaw County. He has performed his work all over the country, and has taught poetry workshops to thousands of young people in schools, juvenile detention centers, and synagogues.

Mary Jeselnick Koral (page 75) grew up in the Pennsylvania outback, rural northwestern country. She has published in *Santa Monica Review, Denver Quarterly, Cream City Review,* and other journals. *Glimmer Train* placed her among the top twenty-five in their fiction contest in 2005. "Broken Glass" is an excerpt from her memoir of adoption and its aftermath, *Thicker Than Water.*

Vicki Lawrence (page 6) has been a freelance writer and editor in Ann Arbor for many years. She has been widely published. She is currently managing editor of the Michigan Quarterly Review and has an MFA from Bennington College.

Chris Lord (pages 28, 110, 121) is editor of the on-line *Bear River Review* and the *Bear River Writers Respond to War* print edition. Her poetry has appeared in several journals, won 1st place in three Ann Arbor *Current* poetry contests, and placed in several other competitions. Chris' chapbook *Field Guide to Luck* was recently published by Pudding House Publications. She founded Word'n Woman Press in March of 2007. Chris is co-host of Writers Reading at Sweetwaters.

Chris Moriarty (page 106) is a student at Pioneer High School and a member of the Volume Youth Poetry Project. His work recently appeared in Washtenaw Community College's *Blood Orange.*

Michael Moriarty (pages 86, 88) is a writing tutor at Washtenaw Community College. He has been published in *The Huron River Review* and *Blood Orange.* Michael is a member of the 2007 Ann Arbor national poetry slam team and recently he joined the spoken word poetry troupe Ann Arbor Wordworks.

Edward Morin (pages 36, 37) has won prizes in eight national poetry contests and has had poems in over twenty anthologies. His poetry collections include *The Dust of Our City* (1978) and *Labor Day at Walden Pond* (1997). With Ding Tingsen and Fang Dai, he edited and co-translated an anthology entitled *The Red Azalea: Chinese Poetry since the Cultural Revolution* (1990).

Christine Rhein (pages 48, 50) is the 17th winner of the annual Walt McDonald First-Book Competition in Poetry. Her collection, *Wild Flight*, will be published by Texas Tech University Press in early 2008. Christine's poems have been featured on *Poetry Daily*, in *Best New Poets 2007*, and in journals such as *The Gettysburg Review*, *The Southern Review*, and *Michigan Quarterly Review*, where her work was awarded the 2006 Laurence Goldstein Poetry Prize.

Veronica Sanitate (pages 42, 94) is a poet, writer, and editor. She is also co-owner and Vice President of MaineStream Organics. As School Improvement Team Co-Chair at Michigan's largest high school, she introduced programs to promote connectivity, build self-esteem and develop leadership skills. She presented similar topics at the Michigan Education Association's annual meeting this year. She is a Reiki Master and a member of the University of Michigan's Program in Creativity and Consciousness. Her poems have appeared in various editions of *Poetry in Performance* and the *Bear River Review*.

Laszlo Slomovits (pages 90, 91) is one of the twin brothers in Ann Arbor's nationally-known children's music duo, Gemini. Gemini's recordings have won numerous awards and their performances continue to draw rave reviews from kids and parents alike. In addition to his work with his brother, Laszlo also sets poetry to music, and has recently released a solo CD of his song settings of the 13th Century Sufi poet Rumi. www.geminichildrensmusic.com

Sandor Slomovits (pages 54, 96, 120) has been writing, performing and recording folk music for children and families for more than three decades, as part of the nationally acclaimed duo Gemini. Gemini's music has won numerous awards from, among others, The American Library Association, Parents' Choice Magazine and the National Parenting Publications Association. Sandor also writes articles on music and history for a number of publications, including the *Ann Arbor Observer, Current Magazine,* and the *Washtenaw Jewish News*. He is currently working on a memoir of his parents' and grandparents' lives before, during, and since the Holocaust. For more, see www.geminichildrensmusic.com.

Doug Smith (pages 11, 12) is an award-winning poet and editor of the anthology *In Drought Time,* a book of Michigan artists and poets, including renowned writers Thomas Lynch and Laura Kasischke. His poetry has been published in *Nomad's Choir,* the *Washtenaw Current, Fog,* and the *Ann Arbor Life Style Magazine.* He has just completed a novel about Detroit set in the 1980s. He is currently working on a second novel and trying to organize his poetry for a possible chapbook or two.

Rick Solomon (pages 66, 68, 116) is a poet and pediatrician whose writing has been shaped by Khrushchev's shoe, the psychedelic Vietnam War era, spiritual demagoguery, and the resilient suffering of children. Recently he has published his poetry in the *Michigan Quarterly Review, 5am, freefall and http://www.zingermans roadhouse. com/* (*Zingerman's Roadhouse).* His book, *The River Through Your Eyes,* was published this year. Rick is a developmental-behavioral pediatrician in private practice. He and his wife of 35 years live in Ann Arbor. He has two adult children—and a growing number of grandchildren for whom he likes to play blues harmonica.

Kristin Stelter (pages 81, 82) is a student at Washtenaw Community College. She enjoys writing poetry and prose when she isn't acting, and is so happy that she found Writers Reading as a forum to share her work. Kristin's performances as an actress and as a poet have been called "luminous."

Alison Swan (pages 43, 44) is the editor of *Fresh Water: Women Writing on the Great Lakes,* her brainchild. A 2007 Michigan Notable Book, *Fresh Water* collects the creative nonfiction prose of contemporary women who know the Great Lakes well. Swan's own poems and prose have appeared in many publications, literary and environmental, including *Fresh Water* and *Peninsula: Essays and Memoirs from Michigan.* Her poem "Porch Swing," published as a limited edition hand-made book, is included in rare book collections throughout the country, including the New York Public Library, the University of Michigan, and Michigan State University. Her newest work, a personal essay about exploring the Paw Paw River watershed with her 7-year-old daughter, will appear next year in a Nature Conservancy coffee-table book celebrating Michigan nature.

Keith Taylor (pages 40, 41) has two new books out this year: *Guilty at the Rapture,* a collection of poems and stories; and *Battered Guitars: The Poetry and Prose of Kostas Karyotakis,* a book he translated with his friend William Reader. *Guilty at the Rapture* was picked as a Michigan Notable Book of the Year for 2007 by the Library of Michigan. Keith has published a collection of very short stories, five chapbooks of poems, and two co-edited volumes. His work, which has appeared in a couple of hundred places, has won awards here and in Europe. Keith is the coordinator of undergraduate creative writing at the University of Michigan.

Brad Tompkins (pages 104, 105) is a poet, writer, and teacher whose poetry has received recognition in the Chelsea Poetry Contest and appeared in Washtenaw Community College's *The Huron River Review.* Brad's poems also are in his chapbook *Wonder.*

Cristina Trapani-Scott (pages 62, 64) lives and writes in Ypsilanti with her husband, two children, golden retriever and two cats. She works as a features writer and columnist for the Tecumseh Herald in Tecumseh, Michigan. She is the 2003 winner of the Chelsea Poetry Competition and her poems have appeared in *Hip Mama Magazine.*

Suzanne Van Appledorn (page 80) graduated from the University of Michigan when John Sinclair was head of the White Panthers, and Tom Hayden was editor of the Michigan Daily. She works as a nurse at Planned Parenthood, enjoys ancient parents, tiny grand-children, and those in between. Reading, traveling, watercolors, piano, "issues," and putting words together with her neighbor-hood group, the Woodlea Women Writers, are her passions.

Thomas Zimmerman (pages 18, 19) teaches English and directs the Writing Center at Washtenaw Community College, where he also edits the award-winning literary journal *The Huron River Review.* He has been published in over 100 journals.

Charles Zwinak (page 22) has written poems about agoraphobia, married love, carburetors, Ankhenaton, and even the meta-physical implications of potato salad. He is our illustrious illustrator and has designed the posters for Writers Reading at Sweetwaters, which have become collectors' items. Our poster gallery is at http://web.mac.com/estherhurwitz/iWeb/WritersReading/

Acknowledgments

Robert Fanning: "Happiness" and "Crooked Wisdom" are reprinted by permission from the author: from *The Seed Thieves*, (© Marick Press, 2006).

Don Hewlett: "Soul" appeared in *Poetry in Performance 33* and is reprinted by permission of the author.

Esther Hurwitz: "Waiting for the Tea to Steep," first appeared in *The Huron River Review, Issue 1.* "Retail Space for Lease,"and "Poetry Should" first appeared in *Soft as a Beagles Ears.* "Retail Space for Lease" was also published in *Ann Arbor (W)rites.* Reprinted by permission of the author.

Jeff Kass: "Fathers and Sons" appeared in the *Ann Arbor News Other Voices,* Sunday, April 1, 2007. Reprinted by permission of the author.

Chris Lord: "Once Upon Ann Arbor" appeared in the *Ann Arbor News Other Voices,* Sunday, July 22, 2007, and "Blue Lint in the Moon's House" appeared in the *Bear River Review Issue 3.* Reprinted by permission of the author.

Michael Moriarty: "Life Art"—a portion of that piece appeared in "From One Writer to Another" by Charles Avinger. Reprinted by permission of the author.

Edward Morin: "Blue Jays" was previously published in *Manhattan Review.* Reprinted by permission of the author.

Christine Rhein: "Googling *Christine Rhein*" and "Friday Night" will appear in the forthcoming book *Wild Flight* by Christine Rhein, and are reprinted with permission from Texas Tech University Press [1-800-832-4042].

Sandor Slomovits: "Ode to Zingerman's Deli" is a song. It has been recorded and appears on *Home From Work,* the latest CD by San Slomovits and Gabe Bolkosky.

Rick Solomon: "Burning Out" and "Crossing Borders" were published in *The River Through Your Eyes*. "Ode to Zingerman's Pulled Pork Sandwich" appears at *Zingerman's Roadhouse* http://www.zingermansroadhouse.com/. Reprinted by permission of the author.

Alison Swan: Excerpt from "The Kettle," which appears in *Fresh Water: Women Writing on the Great Lakes*, Ed. Alison Swan, East Lansing, Michigan: Michigan State University Press, 2006. Reprinted by permission of the author.